The story of LENZIE

Don Martin

AULD KIRK MUSEUM PUBLICATIONS   No. 17

© Strathkelvin District Libraries 1989

ISBN 0 904966 29 1

Cover design by Isaac McCaig

Published by
Strathkelvin District Libraries & Museums
170 Kirkintilloch Road, Bishopbriggs, Glasgow
G64 2LX

Printed by
Cordfall Ltd.
041-332 4640

The Story of Lenzie

The 'Old' Lenzie

Before considering the history of Lenzie it is essential to distinguish between the two quite distinctively different geographical entities to which that name has been applied over the centuries. The old Lenzie was very much larger than the modern. It embraced all the countryside from Kirkintilloch right over to Cumbernauld. The name 'Lenzie' only came to be applied to the more specific locality immediately to the south of Kirkintilloch as recently as 1867. So Lenzie as we know it today is not much more than a century old.

The original Lenzie, extending from Kirkintilloch to Cumbernauld, was a feudal barony belonging to the Comyn family. We don't know when the name 'Lenzie' first came to be used, nor do we know when the Comyns first came to the district, but we do know that the family were established as barons of Lenzie by the twelfth century. They built a castle at Kirkintilloch in the vicinity now known as 'The Peel'. Then, in the year 1211 A.D., King William the Lion granted a charter to William Comyn, Baron of Lenzie, giving him the right to establish a burgh at Kirkintilloch, with a weekly market held on Thursdays. It should be noted that 'Lenzie' was a more important geographical designation than 'Kirkintilloch' at this date. The new *burgh* of Kirkintilloch was established within the *barony* of Lenzie. The Comyn family, as is well known, fell from favour during the time of Robert the Bruce. Bruce, of course, murdered John Comyn ('The Red Comyn') at Dumfries in February 1306.

Kirkintilloch Castle, however, remained in English hands for some years afterwards. It is recorded that Bishop Wishart of Glasgow, during this period, obtained some timber from the English to repair the bell-tower of Glasgow Cathedral, but used it instead to make siege engines to attack Kirkintilloch Castle on Bruce's behalf. After the Comyns fell from favour the Barony of Lenzie passed into the hands of the Fleming family. Whereas the Comyns had been associated with the Sheriffdom of Stirling, Sir Malcolm Fleming, one of the early Flemings of Lenzie, was Sheriff of Dumbarton. So, about the middle of the fourteenth century he engineered the transfer of Lenzie Parish from Stirlingshire to Dumbartonshire. This was the origin of the famous detached portion of Dumbartonshire. Stirlingshire, incidentally, did quite well out of the deal. No fewer than eight parishes – Baldernock, Campsie, Fintry, Strathblane, Killearn, Balfron, Drymen and Buchanan – were transferred to Stirlingshire in exchange for the single parish of Lenzie.

The boundaries of Lenzie Parish correspond exactly with the Barony of Lenzie. The first parish church of Lenzie was known as St. Ninian's and was situated at the Old

Aisle, where the cemetery is now located. Sometime prior to the year 1195 the Comyns presented the Church of St. Ninian's to the Abbey of Cambuskenneth, near Stirling. It came under the ecclesiastical jurisdiction of Cambuskenneth for several centuries thereafter. As far as is known there was never much of a population settlement at the Old Aisle during mediaeval times, so the siting of the church was not really very convenient. In addition, the old St. Ninian's Church seems to have been too small for the congregation, especially after the Reformation. So, in 1644, a new Parish Church of Lenzie was opened in the town of Kirkintilloch. This was the well-known 'Auld Kirk' of Kirkintilloch, now the local museum. It should always be remembered that the old parish of Lenzie extended right over as far as Cumbernauld and included the village there. The people of Cumbernauld were never very happy about the fact that their parish church was at the Old Aisle, almost at the opposite extreme of the parish. The opening of a new parish church in the town of Kirkintilloch in 1644, to replace the Old Aisle church, seems for them to have been the last straw. So, five years later, in 1649, by a decree of the Commissioners for the Plantation of Kirks, the old parish of Lenzie was divided into two new parishes – Wester Lenzie (the parish church for which was

Belfry on the site of the original Parish Church of Lenzie, at the Old Aisle.

the Auld Kirk of St. Mary's in Kirkintilloch, built in 1644) and Easter Lenzie, for which a new parish church was erected at Cumbernauld, being a re-building of a former chapel, soon afterwards. During the following century the parishes of Easter and Wester Lenzie came to be known as Cumbernauld and Kirkintilloch respectively, but the old names lingered long afterwards and reference can be found to 'the Lenzie parishes' at least as late as 1839. The church built at Cumbernauld is still in use for worship today. It has many architectural points in common with the 'Auld Kirk' of Kirkintilloch, which in many respects can be regarded as its twin.

As is fairly well known the correct pronunciation of Lenzie is LEN-YE, which was often corrupted to LING-YE (pronounced similarly to Menzies). The pronunciation LING-YE-MILL for Lenziemill, near Cumbernauld, is sometimes heard, even today. In fact the letter which came after the 'n' in 'Lenzie' was neither a 'z' nor a 'y', but the old letter *yogh* (ȝ), which was pronounced as a consonant 'y'. Because it looked something like a tailed 'z' it was sometimes rendered as a 'z' in manuscripts, and later on by early Scottish printers, who in fact represented the two sounds 'y' and 'z' by the same characters. Etymology is always a difficult path to tread, but 'Lenzie' is usually stated to derive from the Gaelic *lèana*, a swampy plain. A great many spelling variants of the name are found in old documents.

Before the Railway

When the great Railway Age came to pass and the first main-line railway between Edinburgh and Glasgow was made, a symbolic act of great significance for the locality we now know as Lenzie was perpetrated. The Irish navvies cut a deep swath through the Mountain Moss, that seemingly impenetrable conglomeration of dankness and dreariness, which until then had determined the physical character of the immediate area. Useful as it may have been to the burgesses of Kirkintilloch, who from time immemorial had cut their peats from it, it must certainly have had a discouraging effect on persons thinking about setting up home. The coming of the railway heralded an era when the environmental influence of the Mountain Moss would be diminished, to the extent that it even lost its old identity, and when a wave of exciting new developments would bring the locality to life in a most vibrant way.

Encircling the Moss was an area of conventional farm land. On the eve of the Railway Age the principal landowner in what is now known as North Lenzie was William Colledge, a Glasgow writer (solicitor) who had his office at 38-40 Dunlop Street. He lived at Middlemuir Cottage (now Middlemuir House, Douglas Avenue) and owned Westlees Farm (also known as Wester Garngaber) in Garngaber Avenue, employing a grieve there to supervise the agricultural work. Adjacent to Colledge's land was the small, independent farm of Middlemuir. Between the road to Kirkintilloch and Mountain Moss the land was owned and farmed by John Shearer of Gallowhill. Also involved in farming property nearby were the local families of Gibb and McCash.

Middlemuir Cottage, Douglas Avenue.

At Gallowhill, in addition to farming activity, there was a small colony of handloom weavers

At the same period the principal landowner in South Lenzie was John Carss, a Glasgow bookbinder, who owned and farmed property at Glenhead. To the east of Carss's land, David Calder farmed Millersneuk, on behalf of James Miller's trustees, and John Baird farmed at Claddens. To the west, the well-known Buchanan family farmed at East Gadloch and the Alexander family at Loch, where there was also a distillery. The lands of Loch and Gadloch were owned by the Stirling family of Keir and Cadder.

At this period there was, in fact, *no* loch! It had been drained away in a remarkable initiative of the early eighteenth century. During the period 1709-1714 William Marshall, a Glasgow merchant who had acquired the rights to land at the loch from local proprietors, originated a scheme to drive a drainage tunnel from the north-west corner of the loch to Park Burn, a half-mile to the north. This enabled land which had formerly been under water to be utilised for farming purposes. Eventually the tunnel became blocked and the loch 'came back'. Some of the vertical shafts which had been constructed at intervals along the tunnel can still be seen on the surface.

As a harbinger of more impressive things to come, a pioneer railway, the primitive Monkland & Kirkintilloch, snaked its way into the district during the 1820s. Built to carry coal from the Monklands to a wharf on the Forth & Clyde Canal at Kirkintilloch, it passed down by way of Craigenbay, Claddens, Woodilee, Garngaber and Middlemuir, bringing with it, in 1831, the noisy clatter of the very first steam locomotive to successfully enter service in Scotland. Down by William Colledge's house at Middlemuir this primitive iron-horse would have been seen, with crazy cross-heads waving about above its boiler and smoke billowing from its lengthy chimney.

The Trains Arrive

The 1841 Census Returns of Cadder Parish provide some startling information. In residence at Claddens that year was a 32-year old English railway contractor, William Craven, with his wife, mother, four children and three servants; also an English stonemason with his wife and family. On John Carss's estate at Glenhead, possibly in old farm workers' cottages, were nine Irish railway labourers: Thomas Ryan, Patrick McGin, Patrick Quigly, Tim Malone, William Kennedy, Patrick Halpen, Patrick Mooney, Paul Collier and Francis Keegan. Some of them had members of their family living with them. Thomas Ryan's family included a young son born in England, indicating that he had very likely been working on an English railway contract before coming to this district. These Glenhead-based labourers may well have been a peaceful-enough bunch, but elsewhere there were sporadic outbursts of violence. In a famous incident at Bishopbriggs on 14th May 1841 two Irish navvies, Dennis Doolan and Patrick Redding, were publicly hanged for the murder of their English foreman, John Green. Green was buried at the Old Aisle. His gravestone can easily be found in the ancient walled part of the cemetery.

William Craven, John Green and the Irish labourers were engaged in the construction of the Edinburgh & Glasgow Railway, the first railway connecting the two major Scottish cities and enduringly the most important. The official opening took place on Friday 18th February 1842, with an elaborate meal for 1,200 invited guests at Queen Street Station, Glasgow. The station was turned into an enormous banqueting hall by closing the open ends of the train shed with huge crimson curtains. As such it would have formed an appropriate and elegant setting for the occasion, being described in its early days as 'an almost fairy palace'. Normal services on the railway commenced on Monday 21st February.

For readers well versed in the lore and traditions of Lenzie it may come as a surprise to find that the local station opened in February 1842 was on the *modern site*. It was known as 'Kirkintilloch' Station and was provided with buildings of a cheap and temporary nature. The company 'agent' at the station was a Mr. David Johnston, who lodged in a cottage adjacent to Westlees Farm, Garngaber Avenue. He does not appear to have been the ideal type of conscientious railway servant. In November 1842 he was severely warned about his conduct towards passengers, while in September 1843 he was accused of misappropriating 'sums collected by him on Account of Goods' and in April 1844 he was censured for allowing 'his supply of tickets to be exhausted without giving the required notice'. When the railway opened the single fare to Glasgow was quoted as 1s. First Class, 8d. Second Class and 6d. Third Class. The fare to Edinburgh was 7s. First Class, 5s. Second Class and 3s. 6d. Third Class. There were three trains to and from each city daily.

It was fitting that the name of the original stopping place should be 'Kirkintilloch', since there were then very few houses anywhere near the station and its principal purpose was to serve the town of Kirkintilloch, a mile and a half to the north. An important consideration was the condition of the connecting road, which was inspected by the company in March 1842, and an agreement reached to spend £50 on its improvement. In December 1842 the Parish offered to pay over £15 to the railway company, being the usual allocation for repairs to this road, if the railway authorities would agree to look after the road. The following month, however, complaints were received that the road and footpath were still unrepaired. The company ordered that repairs on both should be made as soon as possible.

As early as August 1841, six months before the opening of the railway, the question of providing a horse-drawn passenger omnibus between Kirkintilloch and the station had been discussed. In January 1842, an arrangement was made with William Dick of Kirkintilloch to convey passengers between Kirkintilloch and the railway station at 2d. each for a trial period of three months, the company subsidising him to the extent of £12. However, Dick notified the company in April that he was going to stop his omnibus at the end of the trial period. In July the company purchased a covered omnibus for the Kirkintilloch service from Henderson & Co. of Glasgow for £61 10s., also an open one from Carse of Leith at £42. The following month it was agreed that the fare would be 1½d. 'Inside' or 1d. 'Outside' and that 'the Omnibuses be furnished to one or more parties who might agree to work them'. At the same time it was agreed to furnish an omnibus 'to any party willing to run it between Campsie and the Kirkintilloch Station'. In September it was agreed to cover the open omnibus, at a cost of £14, and to erect a wooden shed for the omnibuses at the station, at a cost of not more than £20. The Campsie Omnibus seems to have been put into service, for on 11th December 1843 the railway company ordered that the Campsie Omnibus be run 'in connection with the 3 o'clock in place of the half past 4 o'clock Up Train'.

Of equal importance were the arrangements for the transportation of general goods between Glasgow and Kirkintilloch, by way of the new station. These were placed in the hands of John Clark, the local carrier, and were retained by him for a very long period indeed. His usual practice was to send out goods and parcels daily, in a wagon from Glasgow (Queen Street) to the station, moving them on from there to Kirkintilloch by road. In December 1842 the railway company agreed to provide Clark with a loan of £12 towards a goods shed at Kirkintilloch, on condition that they be allowed to use it for other goods besides Clark's. The same month the company recommended that Clark's goods be taken between Kirkintilloch Station and Glasgow at an average rate of 2s. 6d. per ton, provided that *all* his goods were consigned by rail.

The Station at Garngaber

In December 1844 the Edinburgh & Glasgow Railway Company re-sited its Kirkintilloch Station to Garngaber, a third of a mile to the east (and adjacent to the bridge over Easter Garngaber Road). The affair of the station at Garngaber is a very strange one, since it is unclear why the railway company ever moved it there at all, only to return it to its original site within four years. The station was moved back to its 'modern' location because the Garngaber site was too far east to serve the Campsie Branch, opened in July 1848. But the Campsie Branch had been under consideration from the early 1840s, and was actively being planned in 1844 before the station was moved to Garngaber. It must be concluded, therefore, that the move was doomed from the outset. It seems odd that so much money was spent on expensive buildings, most of which the company was forced to demolish within a decade.

Certainly there was at least one valid reason for the move to Garngaber. A quick perusal of the Edinburgh & Glasgow Railway minutes of the 1840s reveals the determination of the company to generate 'feeder' traffic at every opportunity, by providing links with towns and villages at short distances from the railway route. Usually these links were by road, but where other railways existed these provided an even better solution. It was natural, therefore, that the Edinburgh & Glasgow company should look to the Monkland & Kirkintilloch Railway as a possible 'feeder' of traffic, both from the Monklands and from Kirkintilloch. Clearly, there were some problems with the road link to Kirkintilloch. For a variety of reasons, the Garngaber station site was more suited to provision of a passenger link with the Monkland & Kirkintilloch.

As early as July 1842 John Miller, the company engineer, carried out an examination of the Garngaber site and advised that a junction with the Monkland & Kirkintilloch line was practicable. Negotiation for purchase of the necessary land was entered into soon afterwards. In March 1843 it was agreed to pay Alexander M'Grigor, proprietor of the lands of Woodilee & Garngaber, the price of £80 per acre for 2 acres of his land necessary for forming the junction. It was also agreed to take 1³/₄ acres at £88 per acre from John Scott of Westlees Farm. At the same time it was decided to accept half an acre *gratis* from Alex. M'Grigor for siting the station. In May the company contracted with John Barr & Co. to form the junction line at a cost of £2, 349. In September 1843 it was confirmed that the new station when built would be on M'Grigor's land. In December a draft agreement with the Monkland & Kirkintilloch for conveying passengers and goods to and from the town of Kirkintilloch was approved. In January 1844 contracts to execute the construction of the station house, station-keeper's house and approach road were placed, including £338 9s. for mason work and £307 18s. for carpenter work. However, by this time the company was beginning to lose enthusiasm for the idea and it was nearly another year before the new station and connecting line were opened, on 26th December 1844. At the same time it was reported that 'arrangements had been completed by which the Edinburgh & Glasgow Company were to run carriages on the M. & K. line with horse power, between the town of

Kirkintilloch and the Luggie [i.e. Bothlin] Viaduct, paying to the M. & K. company one half penny for each passenger carried:— the fares charged by the E. & G. Co. to the public being 3d first Class, 2d second Class and 1d third Class'. David Johnston was moved down to the Monkland & Kirkintilloch terminus to take charge of a 'cheap' station there and a Mr. Symon was brought out from Glasgow to take charge of the re-sited station, at a salary of £60. Interestingly, the Edinburgh & Glasgow Railway Company minutes described the new station as 'Garngaber Station', but a note in the margin opposite instructed 'alter' to this name and the station appeared as 'Kirkintilloch' in timetables, the same name as had been used at the first site.

Apart from the horse-powered service from Bothlin Viaduct to Kirkintilloch (M. & K.), a new steam-hauled service between Airdrie and Glasgow (Queen Street), via the new junction line, was established. The trains ran four times each way daily, but an interesting problem arose with regard to them. From the earliest days of public railways, Scottish engineers had seen no need to adopt the apparently eccentric English gauge of 4ft. $8^1/2$ in. between the rails and had rounded it down to the more straightforward dimension of four and a half feet (4ft. 6in.). The Monkland & Kirkintilloch had been built to this 'Scotch gauge'. However, by 1842 English influence was much stronger in Scottish railway management and 4ft. $8^1/2$in. was the gauge adopted by the Edinburgh & Glasgow. Through running between Airdrie and Glasgow was therefore impossible. The new connecting line, though paid for by the E. & G. Railway, was laid to 4ft. 6in. gauge to allow the trains from Airdrie to ascend to Garngaber. The passengers then had to de-train and cross the platform to join a 'standard gauge' train for Glasgow. This situation prevailed until July 1847, when the Monkland & Kirkintilloch changed its line to 4ft. $8^1/2$in. From the 28th of that month passengers were conveyed right through from Airdrie to Glasgow without change of train.

According to a tradition recorded by Mr. James F. McEwan, passengers wishing to join the horse-drawn service to Kirkintilloch (M. & K.) descended a flight of steps to the low level at the Bothlin Viaduct. The Edinburgh & Glasgow directors were never very happy about this service. They cannot have been reassured by an incident during its first week when a passenger who had positioned himself on the footboard outside one of the carriages fell off and sprained his ankle. By March 1846 the northernmost part of the Monkland & Kirkintilloch was being described in the Edinburgh & Glasgow minutes as 'the portion . . . formerly used by this company'. It would seem, therefore, that this service did not last long. A clue to the date of its curtailment can perhaps be obtained from the fact that on 24th November 1845 David Johnston was given notice to leave the company's employment 'as they had no further occasion for his services at Kirkintilloch'.

When the passenger station was moved to Garngaber it would appear that John Clark's goods siding was moved there also. His practice was to manhandle parcels, etc. from the high level down to a truck waiting on the Monkland & Kirkintilloch line near

View looking north from Craigenbay, with former Monkland & Kirkintilloch Railway on right and spur line to Garngaber on left.

the viaduct. The change of gauge in July 1847 brought great advantages to him but it also nearly killed him. He found that he was now able to run his goods wagon from the high level at Garngaber down the connecting spur to Craigenbay, reverse it there and move it straight down to Kirkintilloch (M. & K.). One day in September, however, this wagon ran out of control on the spur line and collided with an engine taking water on the Monkland & Kirkintilloch. Clark was severely injured.

In view of the doubts attached to the Bothlin Viaduct-Kirkintilloch horse-drawn service from the outset, it was important to secure alternative means of thoroughfare between Kirkintilloch and the station at Garngaber. A cinder footpath was established, leaving the main road about 150 yards south of the Gallowhill Road junction. Its alignment must have been close to that of the modern Hazel Avenue. Nearer the station it followed the course of the Forth & Clyde Canal feeder. For part of its course it ran through Bailie Dalrymple's turnip field, causing that magistrate a great deal of worry over the possibility of theft of his crop. The Campsie omnibus also continued after the move to Garngaber. It was operated at this period by Sandy Taylor of the Eagle Inn, Cowgate, Kirkintilloch (beside Townhead Bridge). A stop was made at the Inn for payment of fares and refreshment of passengers. In July 1845 Taylor was in trouble with the Office of Stamps & Taxes for non-payment of passenger duty on this service.

Campsie Junction — the Station

A branch line from near the E. & G. Kirkintilloch Station to Campsie was originally planned very early in the 1840s, but was left in abeyance for a year or two. The plan was revived during 1844, ironically while the new station at Garngaber was under construction. The company's half-yearly report, published during August 1844, contained the following:

> In the last Report, it was stated that the Directors were in treaty with the Monkland & Kirkintilloch Railway, for a right of way over that line to Kirkintilloch. At the same time they foresaw that the arrangements would be attended with certain disadvantages, and had some doubts as to the satisfactory working of it. It had long been a question at the Board, whether it would not be more expedient for this company at once to form their Campsie Branch, for a part of which Notices were given and Plans deposited two years ago. As this Branch would actually pass through Kirkintilloch, the Passengers and Goods to and from that thriving town would thereby be afforded the greatest possible accommodation.

Arrangements for construction of the Campsie Branch were proceeded with forthwith.

Range of north-side buildings at Lenzie Station, now demolished.

With the discontinuation of the Bothlin Viaduct service in 1845 and the standardisation of the Monkland & Kirkintilloch gauge in 1847 the reasons for the Garngaber siting disappeared. The way was now clear to move the station back to its original site, as soon as the Campsie Branch was ready for opening. This came about in the summer of 1848. On 5th July trains began running to Lennoxtown, and simultaneously the Garngaber station was closed and the earlier station re-opened. The Campsie Branch junction was situated immediately to the east of this station, which could thus be served by Glasgow-Lennoxtown trains.

After the station was moved back to its 'modern' site it was known as 'Kirkintilloch Junction' for about a year and a half, but towards the end of 1849 it was renamed 'Campsie Junction'. The station agent at this period was Thomas Hattersley, later John Brock. The substantial stone buildings on the north side of the line, which lasted until the 1970s, were built soon after the move. In February 1849 the company contracted with Messrs. Herbertson to erect a station building for £828. A year later another contract was placed, with a Mr. William Lawrie, for the erection of a cottage at the station for £56. In August 1850 Mr. James Lamb of Glasgow was contracted to erect houses at Campsie Junction for £236 10s. The following month Mr. Lawrie was awarded a contract to form a well at the station for £7. The extensive nature of the buildings erected at this period is reflected in the number of residents of the 'Station House' recorded in the census returns for 1851: John Brock, Railway Agent, and his wife and family, plus three porters and their respective families — a total of 16 persons.

With the closure of the station at Garngaber and the commissioning of substantial buildings at the new junction station, it was incumbent on the railway company to decide what to do with the buildings on the redundant site. In January 1849 it was agreed 'to convert the Old Kirkintilloch Station House into a Dwelling House'. In May it was further agreed 'to let the old Kirkintilloch Station to the Contractor of Permanent way at a Rent of £10'. On the 22nd of that month an offer by a Mr. P. W. Muir to pay £10 per annum for 'the Cottage at the Old Kirkintilloch Station', when the station agent moved to the new buildings at the junction was considered. It was decided instead to lease it to a Mr. Aitken. However, these plans were destined to failure, for in June 1849 Alexander M'Grigor, who must have been quietly fuming all this while, decided to act. The E. & G. Directors' Minutes of 19th June record the following:

> Read letter of 13th from Mr Alexander MacGrigor, 52, George Square, Glasgow, stating that as the Company had discontinued the stoppage of trains at the old Kirkintilloch Station, he now required restoration of the ground he had gratuitously given for purposes of the station. — Read also a report from Messrs Bannatyne and Kirkwood on the subject. — from which it appeared that Mr. McGrigor had given the ground (to the extent of about half an acre) for the Station and Station Agents House gratuitously — prohibiting the company from using it for any other purpose whatever. — secretary instructed to state that if McGrigor insists upon restricting the use of the ground, it will

be done, but that as the Company would prefer to have its free use they are willing to pay at the same rate as was given for the other ground acquired from Mr. McGrigor vizt. £80 per acre.

M'Grigor was having none of it. He replied immediately, declining the offer, and insisting on the restoration of his ground. Another letter in a similar vein was sent on 2nd July, and on the 24th of that month he wrote to the railway company threatening legal action if the ground was not immediately restored to him. The E. & G. Directors then requested the company secretary to procure an estimate for removing the houses on the ground and intimate to M'Grigor that this had been done. However, they do not seem to have given up hope of retaining the ground, for on 16th October 1849 they 'agreed to let Mr. Aytoun the Contractor of Way have the Porters house at the Old Kirkintilloch Station included in his present rent'.

The matter took some considerable time to resolve, with the railway company continuing to entertain hopes that M'Grigor would eventually agree to sell his land and allow the buildings there to continue. In June 1850, however, it was agreed to 'remove one of the cottages at the old Kirkintilloch Station to Kirkintilloch'. In September 1850 they agreed in principle to pay M'Grigor rent of the station ground, backdated to the closure of the station, but were in dispute with him over the amount he had claimed. Finally, in March 1851, they 'agreed to pay the sum of £25 for levelling the ground on which the old Kirkintilloch Station House was built upon and the road leading therefrom.'

Campsie Junction — the Village

The original idea of creating a commuter village in the locality now known as Lenzie probably belongs to our friend Alexander M'Grigor. On 14th August 1841, six months before the Edinburgh & Glasgow Railway opened to traffic, his law firm of M'Grigor, Murray & M'Grigor placed an advertisement in the Glasgow press as follows:

> DESIRABLE VILLA GROUND NEAR GLASGOW
> TO BE FEUED
> PART OF THE LANDS OF GARNGABER, contiguous to the Kirkintilloch Station on the Edinburgh and Glasgow Railway. The lands are delightfully situated, and, when the Railway is in operation, *will be reached in about one quarter of an hour from George Square.*
> Apply to M'GRIGOR, MURRAY, and M'GRIGOR, 52, George Square. Glasgow, 14th August, 1841.

M'Grigor's lands were at Woodilee and Garngaber, so it is clear that his gesture in providing free ground for a station at the latter place was not primarily one of philanthropy or public-spiritedness. It was clearly an *entrepreneurial initiative*. His fury when the station was moved back west again can readily be appreciated. Examining the remains of early Lenzie 'on the ground' at the present time it is tempting to conclude that the 'Seven Sisters' must have been built at the time when the station was located at Garngaber, to benefit from its close proximity. Unfortunately, this was not so. The 'Seven Sisters' are of later date. If they had been built during the 1840s then Lenzie might have attained greater fame, in socio-economic terms, for Alexander M'Grigor's ideas were in advance of his time. When the London & Southampton Railway opened in 1838 an entrepreneur bought a farm near the Kingston Station and laid out a housing estate which eventually grew to become the commuter suburb of Surbiton. However, even in the London area this kind of notion was unusual in the 1840s.

Villa building at Lenzie began when the railway station was moved back to its original site in 1848. Around this time a Glasgow grain merchant named William McDonald built the three substantial cottages just south of the railway underbridge, then known as 'Rosebank Cottage', 'Glenbank Cottage' and 'Larkfield Cottage'. By 1851 one of these was occupied by McDonald himself and the other two by Alexander Young, a surgeon and dentist, and Matthew Wilson, an Edinburgh & Glasgow Railway clerk. In January 1849 it was reported to the Edinburgh & Glasgow directors that Mr. McDonald 'the Proprietor of the newly-built cottages near to the Campsie Junction' had requested permission to have gates opening on the line from the cottages. The proposal was declined. On 4th June 1850 McDonald wrote again to the railway company, stating that he had built several houses at Campsie Junction Station

View of Lenzie from Millersneuk, with William McDonald's three 'cottages' on the left.

'whereby considerable revenue is being got from parties resident there travelling along the line' and asking what advantage he might derive from the company for so doing. The E. & G. directors declined to grant him any favour but promised him 'some carriage of material free' if he were to build more houses. It seems clear, however, that the famous 'Villa Tickets' notice had ben issued by this time and what McDonald was looking for was a free travel ticket. At their meeting of 26th June the directors declined to make 'any retrospective allowances'. McDonald seems to have sold the three cottages soon afterwards. By 1855 'Rosebank Cottage' was owned and occupied by James Kirkland, another Glasgow grain dealer, 'Glenbank Cottage' by James Marshall, a farmer who worked land near Auchinloch, and 'Larkfield Cottage' by William Bryden, a bell-hanger who had his business at 112 Buchanan Street, Glasgow.

Villa Tickets

The exact date of introduction of the Edinburgh & Glasgow 'Villa Tickets' scheme is not known, but it seems to have been about 1850. On 21st May 1850 the E. & G. directors 'agreed to issue Season Tickets entitling parties to travel to and from any station on the line at rates from a third to a half under the fares at present charged, and to encourage parties building along the line'. In later years the company claimed that Villa Tickets had only ever been granted 'on special consideration of each case', but the wording of the surviving notice is clear enough. Provided a villa cost £500 or more and was situated within a mile of one of the stations, a season ticket giving one year's free travel for every £100 of the house's value was issued to the owner. These tickets could be transferred to a tenant if the house was not occupied by the owner.

It is notoriously difficult to determine exactly which houses at Campsie Junction benefitted from the 'Villa Tickets' scheme. In October 1851, in response to a letter from Archibald Kerr, Writer, Glasgow, on behalf of a client who intended building two 'tenements' of houses at Campsie Junction the E. & G. directors agreed to convey building material at half rates and to grant a free ticket for two years. In March 1852, after examining the plan of a villa proposed to be erected at Campsie Junction by a Mr. Monro [sic] of Glasgow at a rent of £60 per annum, the directors agreed to give a free ticket for five years 'for this class of villas'.

Neither of these applications can easily be traced to a specific property in Lenzie. The villas built at this period consisted, in the main, of 'Bochara House' (later 'The Tower') at the corner of Garngaber Avenue, and the first three houses beyond it, all developed by David Marshall, a Kirkintilloch joiner and wood merchant; the two houses beyond this again, put up by John Taylor, a Glasgow wright; two villas on the south side of Garngaber Avenue, developed by a Dr. Robert Tannahill of West Regent Sheet, Glasgow; and two pairs of semi-detached houses in Viewfield Avenue, which seem to have been developed by Archibald Nairn, a builder.

The best evidence attaches to David Marshall's four houses at the western end of

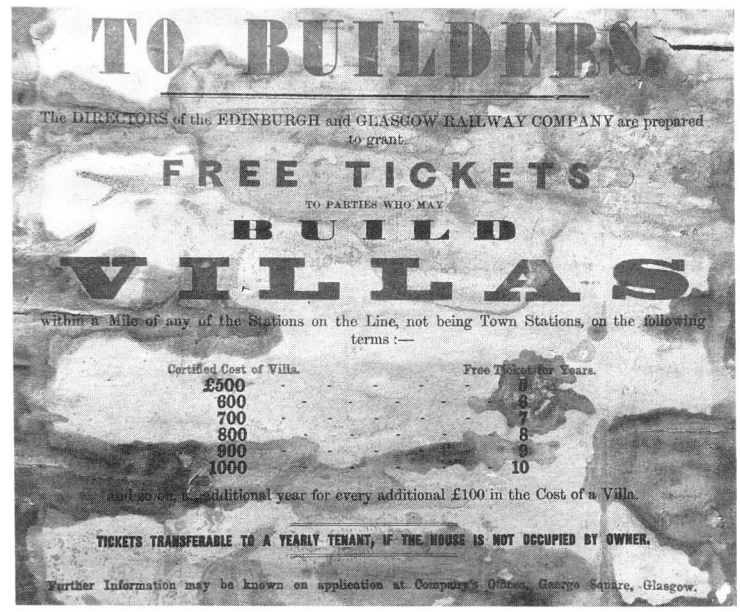

The original 'Villa Tickets' promotion, c. 1850.

Semi-detached villa of the early 1850s. Viewfield Avenue.

Garngaber Avenue. The following is from an Edinburgh & Glasgow Railway directors' minute of 4th June 1856:

> *House Ticket.* Submitted certificate from Mr Munro, Architect, stating that cottages at present occupied by Mr Ramsay cost £950 and by Mr Arnot £850. — Tickets to be granted according to scale.

It can be proved by deduction that the fourth house in Garngaber Avenue, 'Blair Cottage', was at that period occupied by a Mr. David Ramsay; also that a William Arnott was in residence at one of the Marshall houses, clearly the third in sequence, then known as 'Auchnapoodle'. On 25th May 1858 certificates for two more villas designed by Munro the architect were examined by the Edinburgh & Glasgow directors:

> *House Ticket.* Submitted certificate by Mr Munro, architect, of the value of two villas at Campsie Junction that House tickets might be issued. — Ordered to be granted.

It would be unfortunate indeed if these were not the two remaining Marshall villas — 'Bochara House' and 'Maryfield', next door — since these both figure in the local valuation roll for the first time in 1858. To begin with Marshall retained all four villas in his possession and made them available for rent. However, he sold 'Bochara House' soon afterwards to the tenant, William Robertson. Beyond David Marshall's property, it is worth mentioning that the next house in sequence was occupied by the Rev. Dr. William Marshall, Minister of the United Associate congregation in Kirkintilloch, who would have had no need of a villa ticket to travel regularly on the railway.

A very important point to be noted in passing is that Campsie Junction was by no means the only station on the Edinburgh & Glasgow Railway where villa tickets were issued. Comparable to the identified row in Garngaber Avenue was a row of houses on the north side of Springfield Road in Bishopbriggs, for which villa tickets were granted during the mid-1850s. In August 1855 a successful application was made by Mr. William Hamilton of 'Blackmount Villa', Springfield Road; the previous year an application had been made by his neighbour, Gilbert Lang, of 'Rockbank Cottage', and was very likely successful as well. The same Directors' meeting which approved William Hamilton's application agreed on an alteration to the villa tickets scheme, whereby 'season or house tickets *west* shall not be given between Polmont and Edinburgh, or East between Polmont and Glasgow'. Before this alteration was made, it would seem that, in theory at least, villa tickets could have been granted for travel between Campsie Junction and Edinburgh!

The Edinburgh & Glasgow directors decided, at their meeting of 12th July 1859, to withdraw the villa tickets scheme, no reason being given. Thereafter applications were usually refused. A request by a Mr. Ingram in January 1861 was turned down, as was one by a Mr. Urquhart a year later. In May 1861, however, the directors determined 'an understanding existing with Mr. Farquhar that a ticket should be given him, it may be done as an exceptional case'. John Farquhar was living then at 'Blair Cottage' and probably claimed to inherit arrangements made with previous tenants. It took quite a few years for the last of the railway company's commitments to expire. As late as January 1871 it was agreed 'to extend Mr. Mitchell's Villa Ticket between Glasgow and Lenzie till Whitsunday 1872'. Mitchell probably occupied one of the three houses on the north side of Beechmount Road which were built by Daniel McCallum, a Glasgow grocer, about 1858-59, right at the end of the 'official' villa tickets period. In the early years they were known as 'Dunrowan', 'Forthbank' and 'Glenbank'.

Lenzie is Named

It was not just the railway station that was known as 'Campsie Junction'. For want of something better to call it by, the village too was known by this name during the 1850s and early 1860s. There is plenty of evidence for this. *Slater's Directory* of 1860 listed several 'gentry' who gave their address as 'Campsie Junction'. The banner heading of *The Journal*, a local news-sheet of the 1860s, indicates that it 'circulated in Kirkintilloch, Lennoxtown, Kilsyth, Campsie-Junction, Miltown, Hillhead, Waterside, Chryston, Tintock, Mollenburn, Moodiesburn, Cumbernauld, Condorrat, Woodhead, Auchinsteary, Auchinearn, Croy, Castlecary, Torrence, etc., etc.' A list of office bearers of Free St. David's Church, Kirkintilloch, dated 25th October 1864, gives 'Campsie Junction' as the address of two elders and a deacon. Several postal covers, dated October 1859, in the possession of local philatelist James Leitch give the address 'Mrs. Kirkland, Rosebank Cottage, Campsie Junction'. However, the Ordnance Survey authorities were not happy that a community should be named after its railway station in this way. Referring to 'Bochara House' the *Ordnance Survey Name Book*, of the period, made the following comment:

> The cottages and villas east of this & as far as Garngabber & Florabank are generally referred to by the name of the Junction but this name cannot be given to anything else besides the object to which it belongs — the Railway Station.

Accordingly, it was only the station that was given the 'Campsie Junction' name on the First Edition Ordnance Survey maps.

This was just as well, for a change of identity was imminent. 'Campsie Junction' was a poor name for a village, but in reality it was unsuitable for the railway station as well. In his book on *Kirkintilloch: Town and Parish* (1894) Thomas Watson made the following claim:

> The name was found to be inconvenient. People travelling from Glasgow to Campsie, on reaching Campsie Junction and hearing the name called out, thought they should get out and wait for some other train. Strangers got

muddled between the names 'Campsie' and 'Campsie Junction', and letters were often misdirected by mistake.

Be that as it may, what finally occasioned the change of name was the extension of the Campsie Branch railway, under the auspices of the Blane Valley Railway Company, from Lennoxtown to Dumgoyne (at first known as 'Killearn' station) in 1866-67. The opening of a station at Campsie Glen on this line highlighted the 'Campsie Junction' anomaly. On 8th August 1867 the directors of the North British Railway (which company had absorbed the Edinburgh & Glasgow Railway in 1865) 'resolved that the name of the station at Campsie Junction be changed to "Lenzie" Junction'. The name 'Lenzie Junction' made its first appearance in the NBR monthly timetables for September 1867.

The following paragraph had appeared in the *Dumbarton Herald* of 11th February 1864:

> CAMPSIE JUNCTION. — We understand that this picturesque and beautifully kept cluster of villas will receive an important addition during the present year. It is said that arrangements are completed for the building of nine new houses, (five to be finished by Whitsunday), one of which will be opened as a restaurant and general grocery. This shows that this rural and healthy spot is becoming a favourite with Glasgow business people as a place of residence.

The report seems to have been somewhat optimistic, though by mid-1865 the shopping development to the south of Heath Avenue corner (later known as 'Post Office Buildings') was partly occupied and two large villas had been completed nearby — 'Glengair' on the opposite corner of Heath Avenue and 'Ardenlea' just along the avenue. All were the property of George Bennett, a builder.

It was during this period that local residents began to manifest a degree of community consciousness. In December 1864 they successfully petitioned the Kirkintilloch Police Commissioners to put up lamps along the road from that place, at the same time promising to arrange for a person to take charge of them. Even more important was the provision of a community hall, as reported in the *Dumbarton Herald* of 6th February 1868:

> Grand Concert in Lenzie Hall. — The first concert of secular music took place in this new hall the other evening. The chorus consisted of about thirty vocalists from a Glasgow choral union. The hall was crowded by a highly respectable assemblage, and the singing (which was conducted by Mr W. Moodie, and accompanied on the piano by Mr R. Buchanan) was all that could be desired. Such meetings give the residenters a good opportunity of associating with each other, and it would be advisable to have such an entertainment occasionally.

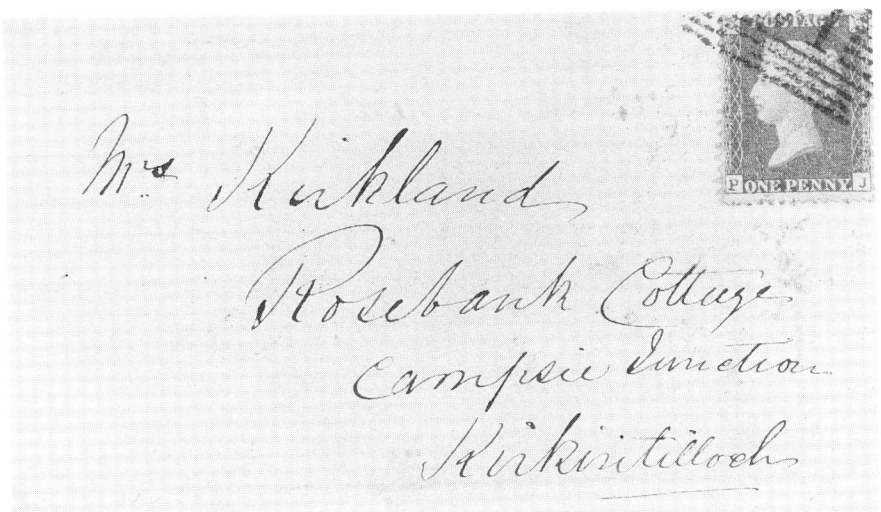

Addressed envelope, with 'Campsie Junction' placename, 1859.

The original Lenzie shopping development of the 1860s.

This is one of the first recorded references to the name 'Lenzie' as a term for the community, as opposed to just the railway station, though there seems to be little doubt that the name came into general use as the local placename as soon as the station title was changed in August 1867.

Further activities were organised in the new Lenzie hall. In March no less a personage than Sir William Thomson (later Lord Kelvin), Professor of Natural Philosophy at Glasgow University, delivered a lecture on 'Musical Vibration' before a good attendance. During the evening he 'conducted a great variety of interesting experiments and showed many beautiful and ingenious appliances in illustration of the subject'. In November the Rev. Dr. Wallace gave a talk entitled 'Our Native Wood Notes Wild, with special reference to Scotland's poetess, Janet Hamilton' during the course of which he 'spoke in glowing terms of the feathered songsters of the grove, and then of the poets of Scotland in humble life . . . '

The Population Explosion

Despite the activity mentioned above, the 1860s was in fact a period of stagnation in the growth of Lenzie. In South Lenzie four houses were built in Auchinloch Road (on the right-hand side between Beechmount and Glenhead) early in the decade, but thereafter there was no further development whatsoever. In North Lenzie, apart from George Bennett's initiative, only a scattered handful of houses was put up. There were few amenities to attract new developers, and there was possibly some resentment that the railway company was no longer willing to countenance special travel deals in connection with the building of houses near its stations.

Everything changed during the 1870s. In the space of ten short years the very limited sprawl of houses, begat by the villa tickets scheme, was transformed into a thriving, well-structured community, an up-market haven for senior Glasgow business folk to withdraw to at night, from the pressures of city life. The population explosion of the 1870s was occasioned by the arrival of true AMENITY, in the modern sense. An explanation of this can be found in a legal document of 1879:

> The village of Lenzie, as it now exists, has sprung up since 1871; and it is only since 1874 that it has become a populous and increasing place, more than half the houses having been erected since 1874. South Lenzie, being that part of the village situated on the south of the railway, is especially recent. With the exception of about half-a-dozen houses, all South Lenzie has been built within the last few years. The introduction in 1874, for the burgh of Kirkintilloch and South Lenzie, of a regular water supply by gravitation from the Campsie hills gave the main impetus to building at Lenzie . . .

1871 was indeed the crucial year. A body of Police Commissioners had existed in

Kirkintilloch since 1836, and operated alongside the ancient Town Council to provide a very limited range of services, but on 18th November 1871 a meeting of Kirkintilloch householders resolved to adopt the provisions of the 1862 General Police & Improvement Act, enabling the election of a fresh body of Police Commissioners, with far greater powers to provide essential services. These new Commissioners immediately determined to give the highest priority to the provision of an efficient supply of piped running water, which could be made available to residents of Lenzie as well as Kirkintilloch — even to those of South Lenzie, which lay outside the Burgh. The new scheme was officially brought into use on Tuesday, 4th August 1874.

Much of central Lenzie, as we know it, was created during the 1870s. In South Lenzie, Glenbank Road, Regent Square, Victoria Road, Harriet (i.e. Heriot) Road, Alexandra Avenue and Burnbank Terrace were all comprehensively developed in that decade. Shops as well as houses were built in Alexandra Avenue. In North Lenzie there was extensive development of Fern Avenue, Hawthorn Avenue, Beech Road and Moncrieff Avenue, and fairly widespread housebuilding at other locations. All three of Lenzie's major churches were established by the middle of the decade, and two private schools were available for the children.

Although the General Police & Improvement Act was not adopted until November 1871, moves towards this end had begun very much earlier. Certainly it became clear during 1870 that there was likely to be a great improvement in local amenities. With this knowledge in mind, activity began right at the start of the decade towards the development of Lenzie into a Glasgow commuter suburb of major importance. Prominent in these early moves was the firm of Murdoch & Rodger, Glasgow solicitors, who assumed responsibility for much of the former Carss estate. Murdoch & Rodger were fairly aggressive in their drive to develop Lenzie and seem to have been quite influential. They were in constant correspondence with the North British Railway Company. On 15th March 1870, the NBR Traffic Committee considered the firm's suggestion that the 'villa tickets' facility should be restored at Lenzie, but rejected it 'as the price of First Class Annual Tickets to that station was reduced on 1st January from £11 to £7'. On 5th January 1871 the Works Committee looked at another Murdoch & Rodger proposal:

> The Committee had under consideration a proposed siding on the south side of the Railway at Lenzie Junction and it was resolved to recommend its formation at an expense of about £150, to be charged to Capital, the adjoining proprietors giving the land free. The Engineer was instructed to see that the siding is made larger than in the sketch plan in order to accommodate Goods Traffic.

By 2nd February negotiations had reached a somewhat different stage:

> The Manager reported an arrangement with Messrs. Murdoch & Rodger as to their siding at Lenzie and the Committee authorised him to take the ground

(about a third of an acre) at £10 per acre and restrict the siding accommodation as much as possible.

Also in January 1871 the NBR directors rebuffed another request for villa tickets to be issued to occupants of Murdoch & Rodger's proposed new houses:

> A letter was read from Messrs. Murdoch and Rodger suggesting that a Villa Ticket be granted at half season ticket rate for each new house they propose to erect at Lenzie Junction but the Board declined to entertain the proposal.

Murdoch & Rodger were directly responsible for the development of Glenbank Terrace (in 1871-72) and Regent Square (in 1872-73). The Glenbank Terrace houses were quickly sold off, but the firm retained Regent Square in its possession and rented out the property to individual occupants. Murdoch & Rodger also collected feu-duty from houses in different parts of South Lenzie.

The Early Residenters

It has been pointed out that during the Victorian era most of the Scottish city middle classes lived up 'wally closes' rather than in suburban houses, unlike their London counterparts who began the habit of commuting at a fairly early period. The nineteenth century villas on the perimeter of Glasgow, it seems, were mostly for 'merchant princes' and the like. Certainly the residents of Lenzie saw themselves as something special:

> The families of Lenzie constitute one suburban community. The heads of these families are, for the most part, engaged in business in Glasgow. A few of them belong to the professional, but the great majority to the mercantile class. The community is, therefore, quite distinct in character from that of the Parish of Cadder, with its agricultural population, and from that of the manufacturing town of Kirkintilloch.

Perhaps typical of the early residents of Lenzie was John Filshill, who built 'Heathbank', Heath Avenue, in 1868. Filshill was a manufacturer of confectionery and preserves who had built up a large business in Bridgeton, Glasgow. He soon involved himself in the community life of Lenzie and became one of the first members of the 4th Ward Committee in 1871. In 1875 he was elected to represent the Ward as a Police Commissioner of Kirkintilloch Burgh and continued to do so until 1882. He also served on Glasgow Town Council. John Filshill was a director of Lenzie Convalescent House, an elder of Free St. Andrews Church in Kirkintilloch, and an office-bearer of Kirkintilloch & Lenzie Liberal Association. As a total abstainer he took an active part in the temperance movement. He died in 1897, at the age of 64.

John Filshill. *Robert Forrester.*
John Ferguson. *Dugald Drummond.*

Another typical resident was Robert Forrester who came to Lenzie about the same time as John Filshill and built 'Gleneden' (now demolished) on the main road next to the Parish Church and opposite the railway station entrance. Mr. Forrester was the owner of a very well-known bookshop in Queen Street, Glasgow, where the regular customers were said to include Lord Rosebery. He was also active as a publisher. He served as a member of the 4th Ward Committee for several years and was otherwise said to take 'more than a passing interest in the communal life of the place'. When he died in 1927, at the age of 94, he was described as Lenzie's 'oldest inhabitant'.

Also apparently typical on first acquaintance might have been John Ferguson of 'Benburb', Victoria Road, partner in Cameron, Ferguson & Company, wholesale stationers of Glasgow and London, but Ferguson was anything but typical in his ideas and activities. Somewhat unusually for a *Protestant* Irishman his lifelong obsession was for Home Rule for the Emerald Isle. On his death, in 1906, the Catholic *Glasgow Observer* published a long tribute, which included this paragraph:

> The Catholics of Scotland have reason to regret John Ferguson's death in special measure, for to them he had always been an inflexible and influential friend. Ferguson was a Protestant, but he was a scholar and his scholarship gave him the utmost respect for the Catholic Church, with whose history he was intimately acquainted, and with whose intellectual side he was a reverential student. His relations with the clergy were always characterised by courtesy and chivalry on his part, and in this respect he set an example which Catholics in the mass might be well content to follow.

And this one:

> In the Irish Movement his memory must remain an example and a stimulus, and when Irish nationhood is attained, it would ill-befit the country he served for so long to prove forgetful of the memory of this brave captain who struggled so courageously in her cause through the long night of depression and sometimes despair, and who nevertheless kept marching on, breast forward, until death found him in the hour before the dawn.

In Lenzie he was widely known as 'Benburb' after the house in Victoria Road which he built about 1872 and occupied for over thirty years, until the time of his death. He was remembered as 'a notable figure, tall, and wearing a flowing full dark beard, black velvety frock coat, and large brimmed soft felt low crowned black hat'. He was also remembered for his remarkable ability to spice his conversation with quotation. He had a high reputation as a champion of local causes, including the Woodilee and Ladies' Mile rights-of-way. He was a member of Glasgow Corporation from 1893 until his death and served as a magistrate in the city for a period. His funeral to the Old Aisle was conducted by the Rev. Joseph Johnston of Lenzie U. F. Church and was attended by Lord Provost Bilsland and several Glasgow bailies and councillors.

Railway Residenters

It is sometimes suggested that Lenzie has been pampered by the railway authorities, and has been given special consideration because of its railway-influenced origins. Be that as it may, it seems clear that in its early years Lenzie benefitted from the decision of some very senior railway officials to live in the place. The first of these was J. B. Thomson of the Edinburgh & Glasgow Railway, said to have been very active in stimulating the initial growth of the community. Thomas Watson's *Kirkintilloch: Town and Parish* (1894) has the following paragraph:

> There were then but few houses — possibly half-a-dozen altogether, which had been built before the Campsie branch was made. Fortunately for the locality, however, the late Mr. J. B. Thomson, passenger superintendent of the Edinburgh and Glasgow Railway, took a fancy to live there, in a cottage on the road to Kirkintilloch. He got a telegraph wire from the station to his house for purposes of his own; although rumour said that its primary one was to wire from Glasgow whether he wished steaks or chops for dinner. He did better than that, though, for he got a sufficient number of trains to stop regularly at the station.

Thomson certainly occupied a very senior position in the hierarchy of the E. & G. Railway. In January 1852 (when he would only have been about 26 or 27) he was described as 'Assistant General Manager'. In 1858 his post was that of 'Superintendent'. The house he built was 'Auchindale' in Kirkintilloch Road, between Myrtle Avenue and Beech Road, which later became St. Cyprian's Rectory. Before 'Auchindale' was constructed, in the early 1850s, Thomson seems briefly to have occupied William Colledge's former house, Middlemuir Cottage, with his young wife Jessie.

Three successive locomotive superintendents of the North British Railway, all of them very famous in their sphere, took up residence in Lenzie. Their place of work was at Cowlairs, Springburn, very convenient in the train from Lenzie Station. The first of these was Thomas Wheatley, who took up residence in the villa now known as 'Hillside', Garngaber Avenue, not long after he came to Cowlairs in 1867. Wheatley was the designer of Engine No. 224 ('The Diver'), which fell with the first Tay Bridge in 1879. By coincidence, No. 224 was an 'engineering milestone' in its own right, quite apart from its other claim to fame, being the first of a passenger locomotive type (inside-cylinder 4-4-0) which became virtually the British Standard for about half a century.

In 1875 Wheatley was succeeded at Cowlairs by Dugald Drummond, who took up residence at 'Norwood Villa', Beech Road. Drummond became one of the most famous of all the British locomotive engineers of the Victorian/Edwardian era, as much because of his explosive personality as his outstanding locomotive designs. The most notable locomotive class of his Cowlairs period was the 'Abbotsford' type, a

'Hillside', Garngaber Avenue – originally 'Auchnapoodle'. One of the original 'Villa tickets' houses, later occupied by Thomas Wheatley of the North British Railway.

Goods engine built by Matthew Holmes, at Lenzie Station in 1960 – more than half a century after its designer's death.

refinement of the Wheatley inside-cylinder 4-4-0, which acted as a prototype for many railways in both Scotland and England. Drummond was also renowned for his excellent six-wheeled (0-6-0) goods engines.

In 1882 Dugald Drummond walked out on the North British Railway and took up a similar position in the Locomotive Department of the rival Caledonian Railway. This was the equivalent, for the period, of a Celtic footballer transferring to Rangers! His successor at Cowlairs was the gentlemanly Matthew Holmes, a much more prosaic figure. His period of incumbency was marked by steadiness rather than ostentation, but he built very good engines. Many of them outlived their designer, in service, by over half a century, and in fact two of them are credited with having been the very last steam locomotives to turn a wheel in earnest for the Scottish Region of British Railways, in 1967. Another of them, an 0-6-0 known as *Maude*, has been preserved for posterity by the Scottish Railway Preservation Society. Matthew Holmes' residence was at 'Netherby', Hawthorn Avenue. Unlike his predecessors, Wheatley and Drummond, he took an active part in local Lenzie life. He was a member of the 4th Ward Committee from 1896 until the time of his death in 1903, a Trustee of the Public Halls, and very active in the affairs of the Union Church. He was regarded very much as a pillar of the local community and many tributes were paid at the time of his death.

Churches 1-2-3

It is symbolic of the incredible growth of Lenzie during the 1870s that all three of the community's principal churches opened their doors during the earlier part of that decade — in fact in successive years, 1873-74-75. Perhaps surprisingly, the first to open was St. Cyprian's Episcopal Church, on 7th April 1873. It has been suggested that this reflected the 'considerable number of English people' who had been drawn to Lenzie as a place of residence, but in fact there were very few English folk living in Lenzie in 1872, when the church was being planned. Once the church was in use, however, it seems probable that many Englishmen with business interests in Glasgow were drawn to live in Lenzie because of the availability of an Episcopalian place of worship in the locality. Very likely the church owed its initial inception to the enthusiasm of Thomas Craig Christie of Bedlay Castle, Chryston, Chairman of the Building Committee and a substantial donor towards the original fabric. Episcopalians from a wide geographical area would have been drawn to the church during its early years, although the original Secretary/Treasurer to the Vestry was William Lester, who lived at 'Garngaber Villa' (later 'Airthrey Villa') in Garngaber Avenue. During the early 1880s J. B. Thomson's former house at 'Auchindale' was purchased as a Rectory. Its first occupant was the Rev. Henry Williams Kirby, Rector from 1876 until 1911.

The next church to open was the 'Established Church' (now Lenzie Old Parish Church) on 30th August 1874. This was the culmination of the work of a committee set up at a meeting in the house of Thomas Whyte, at 'Elmbank' (later 'Greystones') in Auchinloch Road, on 11th October 1872. However, the centenary of the Old Parish Church was not celebrated until 1976. This was because the church was originally designated a 'Chapel of Ease' and was not elevated to the status of Parish Church, *Quoad Sacra*, until August 1876. In 1885 the villa of 'Northwood', Moncrieff Avenue, was purchased for £1,500 from Miss Beatrice Clugston, the well-known philanthropist, to act as a Manse. The best-known minister of the earlier period was the Rev. William Brownlie, who was in office from 1891 until 1926.

The last of the three churches to be established was the 'Union Church' — so called because it served adherents of both the Free and United Presbyterian faiths. The congregation was established in September 1873, the memorial stone of the new church was laid on 21st November 1874, and it opened for worship on 8th August 1875. The first minister was the very notable William Miller, who continued to serve until his death in 1902. The first session clerk was Robert Stark of 'Prospect Villa', Garngaber Avenue, who owned the small shop premises then existing in Lenzie opposite the Parish Church. The Union Manse in Moncrieff Avenue, built on a site close to the property later occupied by the Parish Church Manse, was acquired in 1875 and ensconced by Mr. Miller the following year.

The Academy

The first Lenzie Academy was a single-storey private school, established in 1870 at the corner of Fern Avenue and Kirkintilloch Road. Although private it seems to have been something of a co-operative venture — the owners were listed in the local valuation roll as the 'School Subscribers' and the occupier was the 'School Association'. It was advertised in trade directories, to the business community, in the following terms:

> ... The Academy occupies an open and pleasant situation, and is surrounded by an acre of land, specially laid out as a play-ground, so that the pupils have ample opportunities of engaging in athletic exercises and other manly sports during their hours of recreation. The Class rooms are large and commodious, well ventilated, and fitted up so as to secure the comfort of the pupils, and train them to habits of order and industry. The object of this Institution is to provide a thorough training for entering on a University Course, for undergoing examinations for the Public Service, or for engaging in the ordinary avocations of business.

The rector was Mr. Donald MacQuarrie, who lived at 'Pomona Villa' nearby. A report of the annual prize-giving, for the year 1873, is evocative in its sheer ordinariness:

> The annual examination and distribution of prizes to the pupils took place on Monday last. A numerous assemblage of the clergy and gentry of the

surrounding districts availed themselves of the head-master's invitation to be present on the occasion. The progress made by the various boys and girls in all the classes during the past year, reflected the greatest credit on the head-master, Mr. Kerr his assistant, and the various masters connected with the establishment.

Neither MacQuarrie's school nor any other of the private schools which soon began to proliferate were good enough for the sons and daughters of some of the Lenzie stalwarts, as is clear from a petition addressed to the Right Honourable Anthony John Mundella, M.P., Vice-President of the Committee of Council on Education, in 1884:

> For the great majority of the children in Lenzie the only educational provision is that afforded by private schools. These assemble in incommodious premises, and none of them maintain a sufficient staff of teachers. The education which they provide is, consequently, inferior to that provided by the better class of Public Schools; and it is also much more expensive.

At the same time it was mentioned that forty-five children from Lenzie were then attending school 'in Glasgow and elsewhere in consequence of inadequate educational provision in Lenzie'. A few years earlier (in 1879) the Lenzie inhabitants had approached the School Boards of Kirkintilloch and Cadder with a request for them to set up a 'Combination School' for Lenzie. The idea was rejected but the strong will of the Lenzie citizenry eventually prevailed and the Scotch Education Department of the period provided the necessary sanction. A Committee of Management, with six members (three appointed by Kirkintilloch School Board and three by Cadder) was created and the 'new' Lenzie Academy began to function in 1886.

Lenzie Academy, c. 1900.

The new Academy was formally opened on 1st September of that year. The first buildings to be occupied were the old MacQuarrie private school and one of the villas in Fern Avenue (rented on a temporary basis), but work was under way on a new 2-storey erection adjacent to the MacQuarrie building and this came into use in April 1887. The new Lenzie Academy included both primary and secondary departments. Looking today at the present Lenzie Primary School, it appears so symmetrical in style that it seems a fair assumption that the whole edifice was built as one project. However, this was not so. For many years the school consisted of MacQuarrie's single-storey building to the south and the 1887 2-storey building to the north, and it was not until 1909-10 that the MacQuarrie building was demolished and superseded by a new 2-storey wing to match the one on the north. Photographs reveal that the present building owes much in architectural style to the old single-storey private school, even though vestiges of the latter structure have long since disappeared. The cloakrooms, with apartments above, and the assembly hall in its present form also date from 1909-10.

Development of Amenity

On 28th November 1871, just 10 days after the adoption of the provisions of the General Police & Improvement (Scotland) Act of 1862 by the Kirkintilloch electorate, a meeting of 'the Electors of the Fourth or Lenzie Ward of the Burgh of Kirkintilloch' was held 'within the school-room' at Lenzie 'for the purpose of nominating three of their number as Commissioners of Police under the Act 25 & 26 Victoria Chapter 107 . . . ' In the event, the three Commissioners nominated were William Stephen (of Viewfield), John Farquhar (of 'Towerbank', Garngaber Avenue) and Farquhar's near neighbour across the road, David Sandeman (of 'Woodlands' — formerly 'Bochara House' and later 'The Tower'). At the same meeting a Committee was appointed to look after the affairs of the ward, under the convenorship of James Beith (of 'Bothlin', Garngaber Avenue). Thus was created the 'Fourth Ward Committee' which enjoyed a continuous existence right down to the Local Government Reorganisation of 1975. The election of Messrs. Stephen, Farquhar and Sandeman as Commissioners was confirmed at a further meeting of householders, held on 18th December.

One of the earliest issues to concern the Fourth Ward Committee was the width of the road to Kirkintilloch. In January 1873 Messrs. Moncrieff, Paterson, Forbes & Barr, factors of the former Colledge estate, made it known that they would be willing to grant five feet of space off the land bordering the Kirkintilloch Road. A problem, however, was that Thomas G. Anderson of Myrtle Park, one of the few houses then in existence on the line of the road, was at that time constructing a wall in front of his property without reference to the five-foot concession. The Ward Committee were hopeful that Moncrieff, Paterson, Forbes & Barr would exert pressure on Anderson to fall into line, but in February they received the following communication from the firm, much to their dismay:

We received your letter of the 31st ultimo sending us copy resolution passed at a meeting of the Inhabitants of Lenzie. Yesterday the Deputation therein referred to waited on us, and as then arranged we asked Mr. Anderson to call on us. — He did so this morning, and after hearing his statement in regard to his wall we cannot see our way to interfere in the matter. As regards our unfeued ground fronting the Road we will deal with each case as it comes up, for if Mr. Anderson's Wall is not put back no good could be derived from keeping back the wall in front of the other plots . . .

Another problem was that Shearer, the farmer who owned much of the land on the other side of the road, was unwilling to concede any ground. However, in 1877 the Ward Electors' AGM had occasion to record a special vote of thanks to Bailie Dalrymple of Woodhead 'for his Liberal Conduct in widening Kirkintilloch Road opposite the villas recently erected on his ground'. Nevertheless, when the National Telephone Co. sought to erect a line of poles between Lenzie and Kirkintilloch in 1890 it was pointed out that 'owing to the road being so narrow there is little or no room for a line of poles on the side of this road, unless the Telephone Co. get permission from the different Proprietors to put them on the field side of the fence'.

One of the first amenities available in Lenzie was gas, which was laid on by a private company, the Kirkintilloch Gas Light Company. As previously mentioned, the Campsie Junction inhabitants had successfully petitioned the Kirkintilloch Police Commissioners in 1864 to put up gas lamps along the Lenzie-Kirkintilloch road. During 1877-78 a very controversial issue in Kirkintilloch was whether or not the local Police Commissioners should adopt the provisions of the Burghs Gas Supply (Scotland) Act of 1876, empowering them to take over the private gas-works and run it as a

The main road to Kirkintilloch.

municipal concern. The matter was discussed at a Fourth Ward Committee meeting on 3rd December 1877 when the three Lenzie commissioners indicated their approval of 'adoption' and it was agreed to recommend this course of action to the Ward AGM. In the event the good citizens of North Lenzie took the advice and agreed to support this measure, which certainly contrasted with the moves towards competitive tendering and privatisation of municipal services we have seen recently, during the 1980s. The ultimate outcome was that the Police Commissioners purchased the gas-works from the Gas Light Company for £14,000.

The most purposeful improvement in local services during the 1870s was the supply of running water, which came on stream with the opening of the first Kirkintilloch Waterworks in 1874. Very soon a network of pipes was laid across North and South Lenzie and before long most of the villas were enjoying this basic amenity. As well as wash-basins and sinks the residenters were able to provide themselves with *water-closets* for the first time. As yet, however, there was no system of sewage pipes to match the fresh-water pipes, so a problem arose regarding disposal of results of the w.c.-flushing which was now going on all over Lenzie. As a stop-gap measure the burns of Lenzie were employed as sewage courses, resulting in massive pollution of the Bothlin, into which they flowed, and in turn the Luggie and the Kelvin.

One of the first to complain was Thomas D. Sproat of Middlemuir, who in March 1875 wrote to James Low (of 'Lillybank', Garngaber Avenue), Clerk to the Commissioners of Police, in the following terms:

> Dear Sir,
> I beg to complain that the sewage from various properties at Lenzie within the Burgh of Kirkintilloch is being diverted into two burns running through and adjoining my lands of Middlemuir from which at times a most offensive smell is emitted so foul as to be injurious to health and otherwise a nuisance and deteriorates the amenity of my property.
> I respectfully request you to inform the Commissioners of the Burgh of Kirkintilloch that I shall expect them to take the necessary means to have the *nuisance* abated within fourteen days from this date otherwise I will place the matter in the hands of my solicitor to be dealt with as the case may require.

Much more serious was the action of the Parochial Board of the Barony Parish of Glasgow, proprietors of the Woodilee Estate, where they had recently 'at great cost, erected thereon a large asylum for pauper lunatics'. In 1879 they interdicted the Kirkintilloch Commissioners of Police, the Parish of Cadder Parochial Board and several residents of both North and South Lenzie, to prevent them polluting the Bothlin Burn, which they claimed had until recently been 'a pure and unpolluted stream':

> Its waters, where it flows past the said lands of Woodilee, were clear and pure, were well fitted for all domestic purposes, as also for watering cattle, and it afforded the pursuers, their authors and their tenants, a constant and abundant

supply of fresh and pure water for such purposes, and for all other primary uses.

The complaint against the North Lenzie residents was couched in the following terms:

> The main outlet of the said sewage scheme is in the bed of a small burn or natural watercourse flowing from the Mountain moss on the westward of Lenzie into the Bathlin Burn... Several of the houses recently erected at North Lenzie, within what is now the Lenzie district, before mentioned, have drains wrongfully constructed for leading their sewage into this watercourse. In particular the sewage from the house at Lomond Lodge, Lenzie, belonging to the defender, Alexander Pattison, and from the house at Woodlands, Lenzie, belonging to the defender, David Sandeman, is wrongfully allowed to flow and to find its way, by means of drains under the control of these defenders respectively, into the said watercourse, and thence into the Bathlin Burn.

David Sandeman was Provost of Kirkintilloch at this period. The complaint against the South Lenzie proprietors was expressed as follows:

> Several of the houses recently erected in South Lenzie have drains wrongfully constructed for leading the sewage therefrom into streams or watercourses flowing into the said Bathlin burn. In particular, among others, the defenders, James Cameron, Dr. Campbell Snodgrass Smith, and Thomas Annan, respectively own tenements or houses in South Lenzie, the drainage from which is led into the Cult Burn, a stream which flows into the Bathlin Burn at a point at or near the south-western corner of the pursuers' said lands of Woodilee, and the sewage from these houses or tenements is wrongfully permitted by the said defenders, or one or other of them, to flow into the said Bathlin Burn, thereby polluting the water thereof. Further, the defender Peter Wordie is now building some villas on feuing ground at the south side of Lenzie, the sewage from which is also wrongfully designed to flow into the said Cult Burn, and thence into the Bathlin Burn. It is part of the wrongful arrangements of the said local authority for this part of Lenzie, to conduct the sewage of all houses built or to be built there in time coming, into the Bathlin Burn.

James Cameron was the owner of part of Burnbank Terrace, where he also had a joiner's workshop. The Court of Session found in favour of the pursuers, but the whole question of Lenzie drainage remained unresolved until a comprehensive sewerage scheme for Kirkintilloch and Lenzie was implemented during the middle and late 1880s, with a purification plant at Dryfield on the Kelvin.

Even after the introduction of the full-scale sewerage scheme problems were experienced in Lenzie. During the mid-1890s a major row blew up about the offensive smell escaping from local sewers. In suggesting certain remedies William Marshall, the Kirkintilloch Burgh Surveyor, pointed out that in the Lenzie cul-de-sacs 'during the summer months a large number of the residents are from home, the houses are shut up, consequently the sewers for want of sufficient flow, dry up and become foul and putrid, hence offensive smell . . .'

The Kirkintilloch Commissioners were sometimes resentful of the expense incurred in meeting the special needs of Lenzie residents. The nature of some of these needs and the basic difference in character between Kirkintilloch and Lenzie was highlighted in a legal document of 1881:

> The Burgh is composed of two distinct and somewhat different districts. The one district, embracing the "Town" of Kirkintilloch consists almost entirely of Tenements of Shops and Dwelling houses having common privies and ashpits. The other district consisting of "Lenzie" consists entirely of superior Cottages and Villas each enclosed within its own ground, provided with its own Water Closet accommodation and having its own ashpit situated usually in a remote corner of the ground. It will thus be obvious that the sanitary conditions and requirements of these districts are somewhat different.

In dispute was the Commisioners' legal obligation to empty the the 'remote' ashpits of Lenzie. The opinion of several outside Counsel was sought, usually resulting in advice that no distinction, in terms of responsibility, could be made between Lenzie and the remainder of the Burgh and that the Commissioners had therefore a duty to empty the ashpits.

Sporting Lenzie

Late Victorian Lenzie was notable for the number of sporting facilities available to residents. The first to be established was the bowling green, laid out by property developers Murdoch & Rodger in 1873. The Lenzie Bowling Club was formed soon afterwards and took full possession of the green in 1875. Many prominent Lenzie people were associated with the Bowling Club in its early years. The first President, in 1874, was Commissioner William Stephen (of Viewfield) and the following year the President was another Fourth Ward Police Commissioner, John Farquhar (of 'Towerbank'). In 1879 the principal office-bearer was David Sandeman (of 'Woodlands'), Provost of Kirkintilloch.

A very notable sport was cricket, well-established at Millersneuk by the mid-1880s. Lenzie Cricket Club had two flourishing elevens who travelled widely over West and Central Scotland to play matches. In 1887 the Club was vigorous enough to appoint a *professional*, by the name of Earps. Earps was usually referred to simply as 'Earps', without initials, for example in the batting and bowling averages, to distinguish him from the 'gentlemen'. On 15th June 1887 the *Kirkintilloch Herald* published a touching little paragraph, relating to the Lenzie Cricket Club:

> PRESENTATION OF A FLAG AND STAFF.—On Saturday afternoon, Mr Erskine, in name of the ladies of Lenzie, presented a flagstaff and flag to the local cricket club. In the course of a happy speech Mr Erskine said the ladies of Lenzie enjoyed very much the opportunity of witnessing the cricket matches played on Saturdays, and as some return for that enjoyment they desired to present a flagstaff and flag to the club. On his request Miss P. Boston and Miss Forrest gracefully hoisted the flag, amidst the cheers of the cricketers and spectators. Mr Archer on behalf of the club, in suitable terms, accepted the much-prized gift and thanked the ladies for their opportune kindness. He asked for three cheers for the contributary [sic] ladies and for the two ladies who had so gracefully pulled the flag to the top of the staff.

The demure ladies of Lenzie were unable to speak for themselves, it seems, and were obliged to appoint a male spokesman on their behalf. However, they may have had ulterior motives in their enthusiasm for the gentlemen and their cricket, for soon afterwards the 'Lenzie Cricket Club' became the 'Lenzie Cricket & Tennis Club', with a flourishing ladies' tennis section. The tennis courts at Millersneuk were formally opened on 15th May 1888. The event was reported by 'Wicket-Keeper', cricket correspondent of the *Kirkintilloch Herald*, in the following terms:

> The tennis courts, which were formally opened by the genial president of the Club, Mr Dempster, will compare favourably with the best courts in the West of Scotland. They are composed of red ash, and measure 160 by 110 feet, while the cost has, I believe, been about £120. A nice pavilion, with ladies' and gentlemen's apartments, occupies the northern end of the courts, and altogether the work of laying them out reflects the greatest credit on the professional, W. E. Earps.

The enthusiasm of 'Wicket-Keeper' for tennis did not last long. On 20th June he penned the following:

> The game of tennis goes merrily on from early morn till dewy eve. The courts at Millersneuk are besieged by large numbers of male and female players. The game seems to be very enjoyable to those engaged, but to me it has very little charm, especially when I see that it is playing such sad havoc with the cricket practice, but, as the saying goes, every dog has its day, so I hope will the tennis. Don't stop tennis, gentlemen, but do give a little more time to cricket while it lasts.

One aspect of the local tennis scene did appeal to 'Wicket-Keeper', as can be noted from his report of 29th May 1889:

37

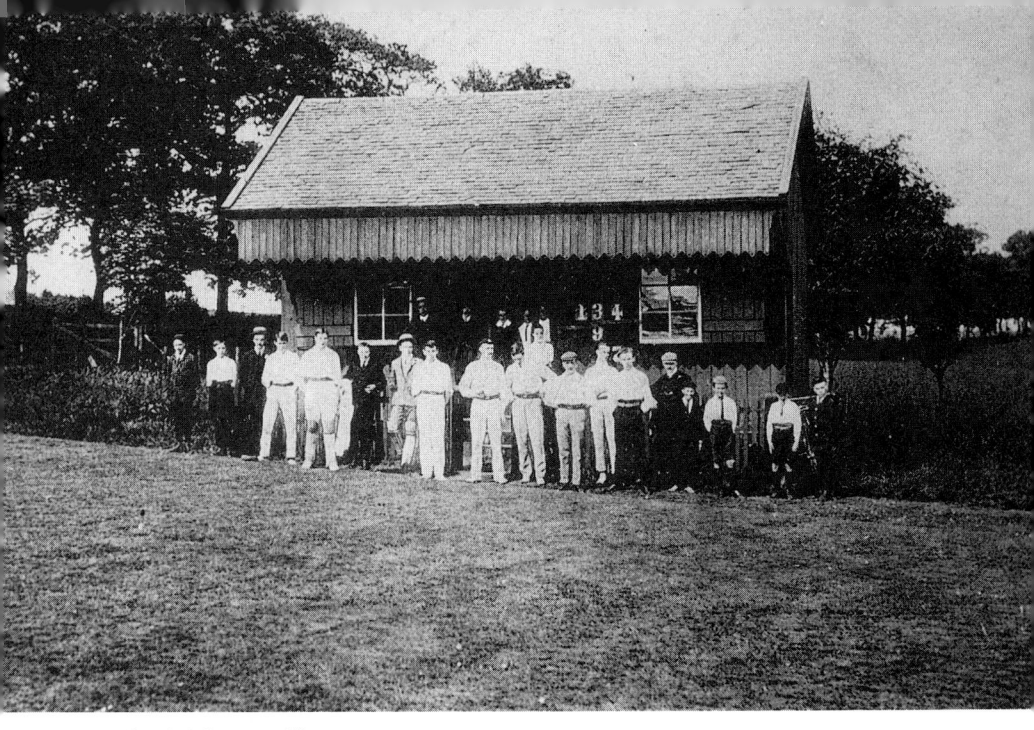

The Cricket Pavilion.

The Tennis Pavilion.

A model refreshment department has been inaugurated lately in connection with the tennis section. The lady members have the management of it, and for the small sum of one shilling per month I believe the members can be supplied with a cup of the finest Pekoe. The members of the Partickhill club were treated to a cup on Thursday night, and seemed to enjoy it very much. Could this not be extended to the visiting cricket teams on Saturdays?

Worries about tennis supplanting cricket in degree of popularity were, it seems, well founded. In 1894 it was observed that the Tennis Club, which had started 'as an appendage to the Cricket Club' had grown apace 'till the contrast between the thronged tennis courts and the sometimes deserted cricket field must have led the onlooker to the conclusion that in this case the tail wagged the dog'. By this date a pair of handsome pavilions at Millersneuk, one for Tennis and one for Cricket, had replaced 'the two sentry boxes that did duty as houses on the lawn tennis and cricket ground' and which 'detracted from the aesthetic appearance of Millersneuk, and were an offence to the people of Lenzie, as well as a considerable source of trouble to those who used them'. The old tennis hut had been 'reminiscent of a weather-beaten bathing-box'. However, the two new pavilions created a debt of £200 and it was the Tennis Club who took the lead in attempting to eliminate this, by organising a grand 'Sale of Work' in the Public Halls on 19th and 20th October 1894. This was a major occasion in the community life of Lenzie and merited a lengthy report in the *Kirkintilloch Herald*, of which the following is an extract:

In a corner was Edison's marvellous phonograph, where for the modest sum of one penny the listener was regaled with a comic song by some bright and particular star of the halls, a military band, or a cornet solo, followed by a reproduction of the plaudits of the audiences who had the privilege of hearing the respective original performances. Beside the phonograph stood a fine platform weighing machine, where the bazaar patrons could ascertain their gross weight on entering and afterwards their nett weight as with depleted pockets they quitted the hall. On the platform the famous Kay family orchestra discoursed sweet music, and beside them was the 'wheel of fortune' in which the raffle tickets were duly mixed and from which the lucky numbers were drawn.

Around 9.30 p.m. on the Saturday night it was announced that a total of £235 had been raised at the 'Sale of Work' (£144 10s on the first day and £90 10s on the second), enough to eliminate the debt on the pavilions.

Association football was also popular in Lenzie in the late Victorian period. It seems that there was both a 'Senior' team and a 'Junior' team. The Senior team faded out of existence around 1889-90. Its ground was known as Craigmillar Park. This may have been opposite the Convalescent Home (on land now incorporated in the golf course) where the 'Seniors' are reputed to have played their final game. Shortly before the

The Tennis Courts.

Sporting Lenzie – with a difference! Sledgers on Alma hill.

'Seniors' gave up some local teenage boys formed 'Lenzie Juniors', a team which enjoyed great popularity for a period. Their first pitch was at Middlemuir, later moving to Myrtle Park. The 'Seniors' and 'Juniors' overlapped sufficiently to have played each other. On 8th February 1889 the Seniors won by eight goals to five at Craigmillar Park. Rugby football came later to Lenzie than the other code, though Lenzie Rugby Club were in existence by 4th March 1899, when they were defeated 12 points to nil by the Clydesdale Second XV at Titwood.

The year 1889 was a most significant one in the sporting history of Lenzie, for it was then that Lenzie Golf Club was founded. The inauguration took place on Saturday, April 20th, when several fields at Middlemuir were adapted for the purpose of the game. Following problems with the lease there, however, an alternative site was obtained opposite the south end of Victoria Road, and a 9-hole course was opened at this location on 3rd October of the same year. A new timber club-house, with a slated roof surmounted by cast-iron ornamentation, was officially opened on 17th September 1892, by Captain John Sinclair, M.P. for Dumbartonshire. Previous to this, an old railway carriage had served for the purpose.

Other sporting events were held in Lenzie from time to time, as for example on 27th June 1894, when a large-scale amateur athletic sports meeting was held on the Cricket Field at Millersneuk. It was under the auspices of the Lenzie Amateur Athletic Club, then described as 'the latest organisation for the muscular development of young Lenzie'. About 480 entries were received for the various events, but the weather was very unkind and the rain descended 'in copious and frequent instalments'. Tug-of-war contests between North and South Lenzie were held at both senior and junior level. The Auchinairn Brass Band 'made sweet melody throughout the proceedings'. It was suggested that this band was then 'more a source of enjoyment to Lenzieonians than to the dwellers in its native village'. Curling was another sport established in Lenzie during the nineteenth century. On 8th January 1887, for example, Lenzie Curling Club played 'a game at points for ex-Provost Sandeman's and Mr. Taylor's prizes . . . in which 19 members took part'.

Residences of Quality

After the great boom of the 1870s, housing development at Lenzie settled down at a more prosaic level. Myrtle Avenue was opened out during the 1880s and many of the new streets of the previous decade were further developed. Into the 1890s the most notable new initiative was the promotion of a high-calibre mini-estate at Grove Park. The developers were Walker, Fraser & Steele, Land Agents and Factors of Bath Street, Glasgow, and they offered the new villas either for sale (at £585 each) or let (at £40 per annum). The great improvement in Lenzie's amenities during the previous twenty years shone out like a beacon in their advertisements:

Grove Park – as originally planned.

> GRAVITATION WATER, GAS, A PERFECT DRAINAGE SYSTEM, AND EVERY ADVANTAGE IN THE WAY OF CHURCHES, SCHOOLS, SHOPS, DOCTORS, POSTAL, TELEGRAPHIC, TELEPHONIC, & BANKING FACILITIES, A SPLENDID BOWLING-GREEN, FIRST-CLASS TENNIS-COURTS, CRICKET AND FOOTBALL GROUNDS, AND VERY ATTRACTIVE GOLF-LINKS, &c., &c.

The 'selling value' of the various sporting facilities detailed above is particularly noteworthy. The Grove Park houses themselves were of note, seemingly tailor-made for the prosperous commuter:

> The cottages are in a very picturesque style of architecture. Each contain Dining-room, Parlour, Kitchen, Scullery, Pantry, Larder, Wash-house, and large Entrance Lobby on main flat; and three good Bedrooms and light Bathroom upstairs. The Bedrooms are fitted with grates, Hot and Cold Water laid all over the house, and the sanitary arrangements are perfect. A damp

course and ventilating gratings guarantee the houses being thoroughly dry. Cathedral tinted glass has also been introduced into the windows with pleasing effects... Each House is detached, and has good-sized flower garden and drying-green, along with a *pro indiviso* right to the large pleasure ground in centre of crescent, which is nicely laid out with shrubs and walks.

Notwithstanding the lack of electricity and garage accommodation, the level of amenity seems quite comprehensive — and indeed seductively appealing, a century on.

Apart from planned developments like Grove Park, many of the individual villas of Lenzie display a considerable degree of architectural character. The merchant-commuters who built them were well able to employ a top firm of architects at the design stage and seem frequently to have done so. An apparent influence was Lenzie resident Robert Turnbull, who was in partnership with the famous Glasgow architect Alexander 'Greek' Thomson prior to the death of the latter in 1875. This seemingly gave rise to the construction of a number of 'Thomsonesque' houses, particularly in South Lenzie, as for example the pair meeting at right angles at the corner of Heriot Road and Alexandra Road. Even in houses where Thomson's style does not pervade the overall design 'Thomsonesque' features can sometimes be noted, such as the gateposts of 'Ballilisk' at the north end of Victoria Road. In recent years the best-designed Victorian villas have been given protection by their inclusion in three conservation areas, centred respectively on Beech Road, Garngaber Avenue and Victoria Road, but including some property in adjacent thoroughfares.

The Public Halls

The amenity-conscious citizens of Lenzie met at a public meeting in February 1889 to consider the erection of Public Halls, of ambitious scale, in a central location. A special committee was appointed and soon afterwards it was agreed to proceed on a plan drawn up by Messrs. Baldie & Tennant, the Glasgow architects. To finance the project it was decided to stage a *Bazaar* in Glasgow and a 'Committee of Ladies' was appointed to organise the stalls and other attractions, with a 'Committee of Gentlemen' to assist in carrying out the necessary arrangements.

The event took place over three days, Thursday-Saturday 20th-22nd November 1890, at the Fine Art Galleries, 175 Sauchiehall Street. Apart from the main business of selling goods there were many side attractions, including a Punch & Judy Show, a horse-racing machine, and above all 'Edison's Marvellous Talking Machine'. Interested people could listen to 'a high-class musical recital by means of ear tubes attached to the phonograph'. There were concerts on the Thursday and Saturday nights, but the concert scheduled to be given by an 'Aboriginal Orchestra' on the Friday night was cancelled, on account, it was said, perhaps with scurrilous fabrication, 'of one of the natives failing to bring his "tom-tom"'. The sheer scale of the event seems to have inhibited the journalists of the period from providing a concise, evocative, account of the main proceedings. The *Kirkintilloch Herald* report included the following:

> The stalls were eight in number, each named after a "favourite flower", and were ranged, two at the east end, five along the south side, and one large stall at the west end of the hall. Every stall seemed more crowded than another with goods. There were contributions from every clime, and of every conceivable description. Indeed, to have done full justice to the wealth of goods a four-days' bazaar would have been necessary. In the west corridor room there was a game and produce stall, where, in the parlance of the trade, a large and well-selected stock of groceries, &c., was on hand. The large amount of articles on every stall was a strong proof of the zeal and energy displayed by the stall-holders and receivers of work.

Travel poster and programme for the 1890 Bazaar.

Much more digestible, if not entirely accurate, was a brief paragraph in the *Evening Times* of 21st November:

> The Lenzie Public Halls bazaar in the Fine-Art Institute is holding its own against powerful competition out west. The pretty girls — all Lenzie girls are pretty — who have no absurd scruples about raffling or fortune-telling drew some £800 from the pockets of fathers and (other girls') brethren yesterday.

The principal item to be raffled was a 'Handsome Walnut Upright Iron Grand Pianoforte', generously donated by Messrs. Muirhead & Turnbull of 101 Sauchiehall Street. Muirhead & Turnbull were only one example among many city businesses and individuals contributing to the cause. In this way the well-heeled citizens of Lenzie were able to promote their personal interest as a *charity* to be supported by the wider Glasgow community.

The Bazaar was an undoubted success, though it did not raise enough money to pay the entire cost of the Halls. In a report of March 1893 the Halls Trustees stated that proceeds from the Bazaar had yielded £1347 10s., direct Donations £564 and a Loan on Bond £700, these totalling £2611 10s., as against the total Halls cost of £3150 — so there was a deficiency of over £500 at that date. Eventually, in 1903, another Bazaar was held and the debt was then entirely cleared off. In an event which almost seemed of secondary importance to the 1890 Bazaar, the Halls themselves were officially opened on 31st August 1892.

Yet More Amenity

In the original 'Scheme for Erection of Public Halls in Lenzie' document, dated June 1889, the following paragraph was included:

> If the Golf Club is the success which it promises to be, it would be certain to use the building as its headquarters, and its Members, finding the premises convenient and comfortable, would be almost sure to join the Billiard and Reading Club. The Cricket, Tennis, and Football Clubs would also be likely to use the building, and from these sources a further revenue of £50 or £60 may be expected.

However, it was not the flourishing sporting clubs who had most to gain from the availability of the new Halls. Rather it was all the other clubs and societies, with a wide variety of specialisms, who gained a mecca for their worthy task of enriching the cultural and artistic life of Lenzie.

First and foremost was *The* Lenzie Club. This Club was formed on 27th October 1892 'for the purpose of providing Reading and Recreation Rooms in connection with the Halls', with an initial membership of 89. Two days later the Hall Trustees agreed 'to let to the Club the Reading Room, Billiard Room, Gentlemen's Artiste Room and Lavatory at a Rent of £26 for the first year' subject to certain conditions including 'No intoxicating liquors or gambling to be allowed'. These restrictions were soon found to be in conflict with the sense of amenity of many of the Club members and eventually the Club passed a unilateral resolution rescinding them. This evoked an immediate response from the Hall Trustees, in a letter to the Club President:

> I am requested by my Co-Trustees of the Lenzie Public Halls to intimate to you as President and on behalf of the Lenzie Club that unless the Trustees within one week from this date receive from the Committee of the Club an undertaking that in accordance with the conditions of tenancy there will be no gambling allowed and no intoxicating liquors used in the Club premises a petition for interdict against the Club will at once be presented to the Sheriff.

This fundamental difference of principle between the Trustees and Club proved irreconcilable and eventually led to a 'parting of the ways', with the Club's withdrawal from the Halls. The Lenzie Club survived, however, and indeed is still in existence at the present time.

Other Lenzie organisations to use the Halls on a regular basis, during the early years, included Lenzie Burns Club, Lenzie Glee Club, Lenzie Horticultural Society, Lenzie Literary Society, Lenzie Minstrels, Lenzie Musical Association and Lenzie Social Evenings Committee. For a period, also, the Halls Trustees ran 'Saturday Musical Evenings', in aid of Hall funds, and the Misses Alexander and Naismyth ran cookery classes.

Before leaving the affair of the Public Halls it is perhaps worth mentioning that the ladies of Lenzie would appear to have been given a raw deal over the matter. The Halls Committee gentlemen were quick to take advantage of their good humour in the matter of organising and staffing the stalls and other attractions at the 1890 Bazaar, which they carried out with notable competence and style. When the Bazaar was over they were supposed to be treated to an 'entertainment' by the men. Meanness prevailed, however, as is obvious from the Hall Trustees' minutes of 8th September 1892:

> The Secretary stated that he had not required to approach the Bazaar stallholders to ascertain the number of Lady Assistants as these were in the "Kirkintilloch Herald" report of the Bazaar. The number was found to be 113 and including stallholders about 150 ladies might be expected to accept the invitation of the Trustees to a Conversazione or other entertainment. After due consideration of the whole circumstances it was decided to abandon the idea of giving an entertainment.

To make matters worse the Trustees then handed over many of the Halls facilities to a club with a 'men only' membership policy! No doubt the long suffering ladies expected as much.

The Public Halls, 1892.

Queen's Buildings, with Post Office Buildings beyond, early this century.

Shopping at Lenzie

The first shops at Lenzie were at the 'Post Office Buildings', built about 1865. These seem to have had something of a chequered career in their early days, but they were given a real shot-in-the-arm by the arrival, in 1871, of the redoubtable Benjamin Mackay. Mackay was primarily a grocer, but in the early days, because of the lack of alternative shopping facilities in Lenzie, his shop sold a wide variety of articles and was known simply as 'The Store'. It was situated in the middle of the 'Post Office' row in premises later occupied as a chemist shop.

Mackay prospered – so much so that in 1887, Queen Victoria's Jubilee Year, he built the magnificent 'Queen's Buildings' to the south of the existing row of shops. As a mark of opulence, these were even provided with an external clock – no doubt of particular value to laggard passengers scurrying to catch a train at the nearby station. The first occupants of Queen's Buildings, apart from Mackay, were James Stoutt & Co., Fishmongers, John McKinnon, Dairyman, and the Commercial Bank. At the same period the shops in the 'Post Office Buildings' were occupied by Archibald McDonald, Bootmaker, John Pettigrew, Chemist, James Mustard, Draper, James Jamieson, Baker, and James Russell, Butcher. Twenty years later, in 1907, the shopkeepers in Queen's Buildings were Benjamin Mackay, Grocer, William Reid, Fishmonger, Daniel McInnes, Plumber, and Annie Jamieson, Baker, while those in the Post Office Buildings included Frederick Sutherland, Florist, John Pettigrew, Chemist, William Robertson, Draper, and William Dick, Butcher.

South of the railway, the row of shops at Victoria and Alexandra Terraces in Alexandra Avenue, was opened up during the mid-1870s. The early shop-keepers there included James Jamieson, Baker, James Graham, Bootmaker, George Anderson, Chemist, John Lang, Grocer, and James Russell, Grocer & Butcher, some of whom later moved over to the 'other side'. It is clear that the late nineteenth-century residents of Lenzie were fairly well provided with shops stocking the basic necessities of day-to-day living, and would not have been over-dependent on neighbouring Kirkintilloch.

Odds & Ends

The founding of Lenzie Hospital, originally the 'Glasgow Convalescent Home', owed much to the enthusiasm and generosity of local philanthropist Miss Beatrice Clugston. The foundation stone was laid on 28th August 1871 by the Earl of Shaftesbury and a substantial building was erected to the design of architect James Thomson, at a cost of £6,685. The first patients were admitted on 31st January 1873. Woodilee Asylum is slightly later in date, but also belongs to the Lenzie 'boom' decade of the 1870s. It was opened on 22nd October 1875, by the Barony Parochial Board, to accommodate 'pauper lunatics' from Glasgow. The 167-acre Woodilee Estate had been purchased by the Board in 1871. They later also acquired the neighbouring farm of Wester Muckroft, in order that some of the patients could participate in agricultural work.

When the Barony Parochial Board built Woodilee Hospital they shut off the ancient thoroughfare by which residents of Waterside gained direct access to Lenzie station. This caused great consternation locally. In 1876 James Cochrane, farmer at Duntiblae, applied to the Sheriff of Dumbarton for an interim interdict to prevent closure of the road, claiming that his feu charter entitled him to cut peats from the Mountain Moss and convey them back to Duntiblae by this route. The matter dragged on for almost a decade until, on 29th June 1885, the Barony Board decided to take firm action once again and closed the road by putting on gates at both ends and locking them. On the following Saturday, 4th July, John Ferguson of 'Benburb' addressed an assemblage of 3,000 people at Waterside, then marched before them to each gate in turn. With Ferguson's characteristic sense of propriety, a guarantee was given to the police present that all damage would be paid for, then the locks were forced and the gates declared open. The *Lennox Herald* commented that 'there was no tendency to disorder'. Later in the month, on Monday 27th July, a well-attended public meeting in the Temperance Hall, Kirkintilloch, was harangued on the subject by Ferguson, and also by that other Lenzie stalwart, John Filshill, who chaired the meeting. These displays of local feeling seem to have had an effect on the Barony Board who soon afterwards decided to construct a footpath and bridge, on an alternative course but still providing a reasonably direct route between Waterside and Lenzie Station. The opening of the new route was reported in the *Kirkintilloch Herald* of 30th May 1888, with the comment that 'both bridge and footpath are miserable substitutes for the old road, and neither are much to the credit of the Asylum Directors'. The bridge was described as a 'giddy, shaky, spider looking inclined plane over the valley of the Bothlin'. This seems to be the origin of the 'Spider Bridge' name, although the writer can remember crossing the bridge on a frosty autumn morning in 1981 and noting tens of thousands of spiders' webs glistening in the sun between the diamonds of the iron lattice-work. The loss of this bridge in recent years is surely a disaster for Lenzie. Any locality with pretensions to high amenity should possess a measure of the curious and the interest-arousing, as well as just convenience, beauty and elegance. In Lenzie this measure has undoubtedly been diminished.

On 29th March 1858 the Directors of the Edinburgh & Glasgow Railway considered a memorial from the inhabitants of Boghead for the formation of a footpath from 'that village to Campsie Junction Station'. The Directors, however, 'declined to subscribe'. Nevertheless, the footpath known as 'The Lady's Mile' seems to have been laid alongside the railway, on the south side, soon afterwards. 'The Lady's Mile' was formed entirely on railway property, and so the railway company had full control of it, but in due course it seems that local residents came to regard it as a 'Right of Way'. To remind the public that thoroughfare was a privilege and not a right, and to prevent any legal question of 'Right of Way' arising, the North British Railway from time to time closed off the pathway for a short period by securing the turnstile gates at either

Woodilee Asylum – nineteenth century drawing.

The end of the Spider Bridge, July 1987.

end with padlocks and chains. One such occasion was on Saturday 26th August 1904, when notices were posted that the 'Lady's Mile' would be closed from 5 pm on that day until 7 am on Monday the 28th. The same evening a band of young John Ferguson protégés descended on the gates, removing spars from the eastern one and lifting the one at the Cadder end off its hinges. The railway company was quick to act and on the Sunday morning the gates were secured once more. This time the old man himself arrived and removed a link from one of the chains with a chisel. 'Benburb' no doubt imagined that there were parallels in this instance with the previous celebrated cause at Woodilee, but really there were none – the North British Railway had no intention of closing the 'Lady's Mile' for good. At a meeting held in Lenzie Upper Public Hall on 11th March 1905 it was unanimously agreed to send a letter to the N.B.R., acknowledging the company's rights with regard to the path, including the right to close it for one day each year, but expressing the hope that the public might be allowed to continue to use it at all other times. John Ferguson was displeased, but in this case it would seem that his sense of outrage was misplaced. In later years the memory of her father's defeat over this matter enabled Miss Anna Bertram Ochiltree Ferguson to keep the citizens of Lenzie on the 'right track' when the question of the railway company's right to close the 'station lane' between Auchinloch Road and Alexandra Avenue, for one day in the year, arose.

Glasgow business men usually regarded Lenzie as a place of residence and *not* as a place of work, but noted exceptions in this respect were the Annan Brothers, Thomas and Robert, the famous photographers of *Old Closes & Streets of Glasgow* fame. About 1876 they took over the old Glenhead House as a photographic printing workshop, and later they also occupied premises in Beechmount Road for the same purpose. Thomas Annan took up residence at 'Elmbank', Auchinloch Road. The Glenhead premises were described in detail in the *British Journal of Photography* of 19th April 1878, the reporter being impressed by some very large glass negatives:

> "What do you mean by a large picture?" is frequently asked, and I suppose the answer must always be a somewhat negative one; but here I saw what most photographers would admit was a large negative, being a copy of a picture on a plate seven feet by three and a half feet.

He was shown 'a finished set of 13,000 prints from one hundred negatives, for a second edition of a book about to be published in Glasgow' and was told about another order in the course of execution, consisting of '3,000 prints from thirty negatives of the old closes and other interesting portions of Glasgow now removed by the Improvements Trust to make way for more modern erections'.

In the year 1890 the Lenzie residenters were alarmed to discover that a *coal pit* was being planned for Woodilee, right on their doorstep. It was difficult to imagine a greater threat to amenity. Needless to say they protested, but the entrepreneur, John McCallum, was well provided with 'friends at court' and the plans were passed. No. 1

pit began to deliver coal in 1891. During its forty years of existence the Woodilee Colliery does not seem to have interfered in any really serious measure with the amenity of Lenzie, though workings were opened out under a wide area of the locality. It finally closed down in May 1931, throwing a total of about 300 men on the unemployment roll. In March of the following year there was an inadequate attempt by a *Kirkintilloch Herald* reporter to describe the scene of dereliction, with flowery journalese:

> It is strange how soon disused buildings take on that dejected, forlorn look which denotes the absence of the activity of man . . . A little "puffing billy", whose ironwork already bears witness of the ravages of neglect and weather, sits silently among the ruins. Its importance lay in its blustering voice, and that, alas, it cannot retain, nor can the smoke stack its haughty mien . . . [etc., etc.] . . .

Nowadays it is impossible to find evidence on the ground that there was once a colliery at Woodilee.

The Lenzie Provosts

Although Lenzie was never itself a burgh as such, there were quite a few 'Provosts of Lenzie'. This was because a fairly high proportion of the Provosts of Kirkintilloch, elected from 1871 onwards, were supplied by the Fourth, or Lenzie, Ward. The first, and possibly the greatest of them all, was David Sandeman of 'Woodlands' (later 'The Tower'). 'The Tower' being such an imposing structure in central Lenzie it is pleasing to think that one of its former occupants was indeed a 'towering' figure in the community. David Sandeman was involved in virtually every aspect of Lenzie life, and influential in the development of many of them. He was one of the original Fourth Ward Commissioners in 1871 and was Provost from 1877 until 1880. Like the majority of Lenzie residents he was a Glasgow business man, his firm being David Sandeman & Co., British and foreign yarn merchants. He also had a close connection with the Glasgow Technical College and was influential in the setting up of a Technical School of Weaving there. He was said to be 'an active and honoured member' of Glasgow Chamber of Commerce. He died in 1887, at the age of 73.

The next 'Lenzie Provost' was A.C. Rutherford of 'The Grange', Beech Road, who held the office from 1890 until 1893. He also served as Chairman of the Parish Council and as a member of the School Board. His greatest professional achievement was the development of the West of Scotland Guardian Society, said to have proved 'of great assistance to trade and commerce in the West of Scotland'. The only other 'Lenzie Provost' of the Victorian era was James Stewart of 'Eden Park', Middlemuir, who served on Kirkintilloch Town Council for 12 years and was Provost from 1896 until

Provost A. C. Rutherford. *Provost David Perry.*

1899. James Stewart's business interest was as an 'agent' for the National Bank of Scotland in Glasgow, first at the Sauchiehall Street Branch, later moving to the St. Rollox Branch at Springburn. While at the latter place he served as Clerk to the Springburn School Board.

Lenzie Provosts of the twentieth century have included: Andrew Graham Service (of 'Dalgowrie', Moncrieff Avenue), 1902-8; David Perry (of 'Norwood', Beech Road), 1908-11; John Walker (of 'Eden House', Garngaber Avenue), 1912-18; James R. Rutherford (of 'The Grange', Beech Road), 1930-33; John B. Fairservice (of 'Pomona', Kirkintilloch Road), 1958-61; Mrs. Janet M. Coutts (of 'Medwyn', Heath Avenue), 1964-67; and finally William Leslie, 1970-73, who still serves as a member of Strathkelvin District Council at the present time. David Perry will always be remembered for his gift of a bandstand in 1905 to the town of Kirkintilloch, where it can still be seen in the Peel Park. J. R. Rutherford in 1955 became one of the very few Freemen of the Burgh of Kirkintilloch. Provost Fairservice presided at many important civic functions during his period of office when the 'Glasgow Overspill' was at its height. Mrs. Coutts was the only woman ever to be Provost of Kirkintilloch. She fulfilled an important engagement in 1965, when she welcomed Her Majesty the Queen to the town.

The Twentieth Century

The main purpose of this book is to provide insight into the factors which caused Lenzie to spring to life, from very small beginnings, during the nineteenth century. However, it is not intended to leave matters hanging at the year 1900 – a brief summary of the principal twentieth century events will not be out of place. A notable early-century development was the provision of organised activities for the youth of Lenzie – markedly absent before 1900. A Boy Scout troop was formed in 1908 by Robert Warnock, who was later killed in the First World War. The local Girl Guides came into being in 1920. Many Lenzie ladies were active in the cause of Women's Suffrage. On 16th October 1913 they supported the movement in time-honoured Lenzie fashion – with a 'Cake & Candy Sale' in the Public Hall.

The greater variety of house types erected in Lenzie during the twentieth century brought a broader spectrum of the 'white collar' middle classes to the locality – commercial travellers, school teachers, civil servants, local government officials, bank and office clerks, and so on – as well as further representatives of the city business community. Quite notable between the Wars was the spread of bungalows along the Kirkintilloch Road and down adjacent thoroughfares such as Laurel Avenue and Middlemuir Road. There was also some *council housing* built within the Fourth Ward limits at this time – in Gallowhill Avenue. During the second half of the century, with the development of the various 'estates' and the opening out of many new roads and avenues by large house-building firms, Lenzie has seen a period of expansion comparable to its initial surge during the late nineteenth century.

Responsibility for Lenzie Academy was assumed by the County Council of Dunbarton Education Department in 1918. Thereafter the school continued with both primary and secondary sections 'cheek by jowl' for quite a considerable time. Eventually, in 1960, a new secondary school was opened at Myrtle Avenue and the old school was occupied by younger children only, as Lenzie Primary School. Further primary schools were opened up at Lenzie Moss (1967) and Millersneuk (1978). From 1966 Catholic children were accommodated at Holy Family Primary School, Gallowhill Road. There was a bizarre occurrence in January-February 1935 when over 300 Lenzie Academy pupils were taken out 'on strike' by parents in support of their erstwhile rector, the energetic and innovative George Murray, who by dint of some personality clash had been 'demoted' to the post of Second Master at Vale of Leven Academy. The strike lasted for six weeks, during which period the pupils were given unofficial lessons by retired teachers in the Public Hall and in private houses, but on 18th February the 'strikers' were lined up in procession outside the Public Hall, then led across the road by the Rev. Hassal Hanmer, President of the Parents' Association, and welcomed at the school gate by Mr. Roderick McLean, the acting headmaster, in his academic gown. Sad to relate, the protest was all in vain, and Mr. Murray was never reinstated as Rector of Lenzie Academy.

It seems fair to state that Lenzie people gave their overwhelming support to the cause of the nation during both World Wars. After World War II a very attractive book, the *Roll of Honour,* listing the 366 Lenzie people who had taken part in the War, was prepared and copies presented to local ex-service men and women. An etching by local artist W. Douglas Macleod appeared on the title page and the beautiful hand-lettering was by his daughter Ann. Distribution of the book was organised by the Lenzie Welcome Home & Commemoration Fund and the cost of its preparation was borne by an anonymous donor. Many copies are still cherished in Lenzie by their owners at the present time.

During the earlier part of the century there were, it seems, some very important and well-used shops in Alexandra Avenue. Older residents recall, in particular, the 'spotless' Lahore's Dairy, with a basement below where the metal milk cans were washed, then stored on their sides on a stone shelf; and McLean's shoe shop next door, with a cobbler's workshop in the basement, where soling and heeling was carried out. For much of the century, however, this row of shops has been very much in the shade of those in Queen's & Post Office Buildings, notwithstanding the importance of its licensed grocer to thirsty residents of Kirkintilloch during the long 'dry' period in the burgh. In the years just after the Second World War the Queen's / Post Office row seemed especially vibrant, perhaps because of the bright personalities of so many of the shopkeepers and shop-assistants at that time, such as the smart and efficient grocer John Macdonald, the formidable chemist Frank Arthur, kindly Matt Forrester (bosom friend of the famous Tom Weir) in Cumming the butchers, Mrs. Mercer in the paper shop and Nellie in the fish-shop. Elsewhere in Lenzie important rôles were fulfilled by Maggie McCulloch's 'tuck-shop' next to the Public Hall, 'Bungalow' Joe Henderson's primitive wooden sweet-shop and tearoom on the corner of Lindsaybeg Road, and Mary White's somewhat unusual-looking shop next to the station on the south side, selling papers, sweets, toys, etc.

Going back to the earlier part of the century a most important person in the commercial life of Lenzie was Bob Henderson, the N.B.R. carter, who delivered goods of all kinds from the railway station. In those days virtually everything went by train. It seems that 'Bob' could be prevailed upon to carry out 'unofficial' work from time to time, such as moving chairs and other items of furniture from private houses on his horse-drawn lorry to the Public Hall, for use at dances run by the various local organisations. Another kenspeckle figure was Willie Cameron, of the carriage-hiring business in Garngaber Avenue, one of whose regular duties was to drive the well-known Dr. William Armstrong around in a 'dog cart' to visit patients – in the days before the good doctor acquired a motor car. There were also the various message boys, employed by local grocers, who visited regular customers *every day* to take orders for provisions, which would be delivered the same day. In the earliest years these deliveries were in heavy baskets carried on the boys' heads – later by bicycle.

The Changing Environment

The 'cold, bare and barren' nature of Lenzie before the Railway Age is summed up in a quotation which appeared in Thomas Watson's *Kirkintilloch: Town and Parish* (1894) and has been used on many occasions since. No apology is offered for citing it again here:

> Campsie Junction! a laverock would hardly licht on't.

With the coming of the villas it should not be imagined that Lenzie lost its 'drear' aspect immediately, as if by magic. Much hard work was required to transform it into the attractively laid-out configuration of dwellings, gardens and trees we know so well. Even as late as 1940 John Hillis could detect traces of the old order:

> In several parts of South Lenzie the ground has lain vacant all down the years, ungraced by human habitation, a memorial of tearful melancholy, overgrown with weeds and rank grass.

Nowadays Lenzie is unrivalled in the area round Glasgow for its consistently high standard of upkeep, wherever one cares to wander. A colleague of the writer's, and former resident of Lenzie, recently commented on how impressed he had been on a return visit, and how easy it was to forget just how high the standards are maintained. Even the Mountain Moss has lost much of its 'dankness and dreariness' – perhaps the large-scale extraction of peat during the twentieth century has helped – and is now cherished as another amenity by the Lenzie residents. In High Gallowhill people dwell right on its very edge, apparently without any ill effects.

Excavation of cutting for new road under the railway, beside Lenzie Station, 1963.

Because the railway was so important in the development of Lenzie and always occupied such a dominating situation in the local environment, changes in the railway infrastructure have had a quite noticeable influence. The demolition of the old railway buildings in 1977 (some of them a few years earlier), and the building of brash new ones, seemed to have the effect of driving a wedge between North and South Lenzie, at the very period when, for the first time, the two halves had just been brought under the umbrella of the same local authority. The old station, erected during the same wave of activity as the first villas, had a harmonising effect which has been extinguished for ever. Historically, the north-side main station building was the *most important* structure in Lenzie. The fact that the new buildings are of a higher standard than, for example, those at Bishopbriggs, does not really compensate for the loss which has been sustained.

The closure of the northernmost stretch of the former Monkland & Kirkintilloch Railway in 1966 has resulted in the creation of an attractive walkway along its route between Woodilee and Whitegates. The complete closure of the 'Campsie Branch' at the same time has had an even greater effect on the Lenzie environment – bridges and massive embankments at Garngaber and Woodilee having been removed. It is intended that part of its course will be used for a new high-grade road linking Kirkintilloch with the Stepps bypass, and skirting Lenzie to the east.

Over a quarter of a century has now elapsed since the road under the railway at Lenzie Station was straightened, with the loss of Robert Forrester's old house at 'Gleneden' and the disappearance of the *Mirror* which enabled traffic negotiating the sharp, narrow bend at this point to see what was coming in the opposite direction. The Mirror had a long history, having been put up around the time of outbreak of World War I. Two extracts from the *Kirkintilloch Herald* of the period give some insight into why it was

Bus taking the 'old road' at Lenzie Station, 1963. The house on the left, later demolished, is 'Gleneden'.

deemed necessary, so early in the motor car era. The first is from the issue of Wednesday 7th August, 1912:

> SERIOUS ACCIDENT. Last Friday afternoon about five o'clock a serious accident occurred almost below the railway bridge at the dangerous corner where Kirkintilloch and Auchinloch roads conjoin. It appears that a baker's van was turning the corner towards Kirkintilloch, and that George Jackson, Muirhead was riding a motor cycle homewards. The result was that on turning the corner both parties made a hurried endeavour to clear each other, but were not altogether successful as Jackson's right leg struck the van in passing, and he ran into a man almost immediately afterwards, and rode several yards further on, when he fell to the ground. It was seen that Jackson had sustained some injury and Dr. McIntyre was immediately sent for. He found that the man had sustained a compound fracture of the right leg below the knee, and ordered his removal to the Western Infirmary, whence he was taken with all speed in Mr. Cameron's motor car. A desire is strongly expressed locally that the authorities will try to improve this corner, which Mr. Auld at Monday's meeting of the District Committee of the Lower Ward of Lanarkshire characterised as a 'death trap'.

The other one is from the *Herald* of 2nd July 1913:

> Yesterday morning shortly after nine o'clock, an accident of an alarming nature, but one happily unattended by any serious personal injury, occurred underneath the railway bridge, at the dangerous corner of the road near Lenzie Station. A motor car belonging to Mr. Wm. Robertson, veterinary surgeon, Kirkintilloch, and a milk van belonging to Mr. Steven, Wester Auchinloch, were involved in the mishap. The car, in which were Mr. Robinson, who was driving, and his little daughter, was proceeding to Stepps, while the van, in which was seated Mr. Steven, was going in the opposite direction.

The Mirror (or rather the *first* Mirror, for there were at least two over half a century) can be seen in photographs of a locomotive which had crashed over the bridge parapet, dating from about 1914.

Boundaries

There can be no place of comparable size in the entire country where political boundaries have had such a drastic effect as in Lenzie. The most significant of these was the east-west boundary between Lanarkshire and the detached portion of Dumbartonshire, which had the effect of dividing Lenzie into two approximately equal halves, for all government purposes, a state of affairs which prevailed until 1975. The

Demolition of old Lenzie Station, June 1977.

Derailed locomotive at the station underbridge, c. 1914. The Mirror can be seen on the other side of the bridge.

Lanarkshire / Dunbartonshire county boundary ran from Lenzie Moss eastwards along a small tributary burn, flowing under Lenzie Station and into the Cult Burn at Millersneuk, thence eastwards again along the Cult Burn to its meeting with the Bothlin at Garngaber. Also important was the boundary of the Burgh of Kirkintilloch – or rather *boundaries*, for there were two of them. The boundary of the modern police burgh, dating from 1871, ran from Lenzie Moss with the little burn as far as Lenzie Station, thence eastwards along the railway to Garngaber. The boundary of the ancient Burgh of Barony, on the other hand, ran north-eastwards from Lenzie Moss along the line of the lane behind the houses on the south side of Hawthorn Avenue, passing to the south of 'Pomona' and the Public Hall, and to the north of old Lenzie Academy and Dean House, thence more-or-less due east as far as the Monkland & Kirkintilloch Railway. It will be recognised that there was a narrow east-west strip of Lenzie which lay within the County of Dunbarton (and Parish of Kirkintilloch) but outside the Burgh of Barony and an even narrower strip which was within the Parish, but outside the Police Burgh.

These anomalies all ceased with the Local Government Reorganisation of 1975. Lenzie *in its entirety* now lies within the Strathclyde Region (for purposes of roads, education, social work, etc.) and within the Strathkelvin District second tier authority (for services such as leisure & recreation, local planning, and environmental health). Counties and burghs no longer have any relevance in Scottish local government. At long last Lenzie has been united – not any more does it have a split identity. Perhaps the only question still to be answered is whether Lenzie (the whole of it) is to be regarded as a locality of Kirkintilloch or whether Lenzie (again the whole of it) has now nothing at all to do with Kirkintilloch and can be regarded as a totally separate geographical entity. Officialdom would seem to favour the former version. The Strathkelvin District Valuation Rolls make reference to thoroughfares such as 'Victoria Road, Kirkintilloch' and 'Grove Park, Kirkintilloch', while the 1981 Government Census Statistics group Lenzie (also Auchinloch and Waterside) with Kirkintilloch and give no separate population figures for Lenzie as such. The late Miss Ethel Lakeman, in her talks relating to Lenzie's history, used to end with a plea that 'may the day never dawn ... when ... the historic name of Lenzie is allowed to founder and be lost for ever in the Sea of Oblivion'. There seems to be little danger of this happening, though Lenzie folk may one day, perhaps quite soon, have to decide whether or not they wish to remain as part of Kirkintilloch, in the eyes of officialdom. When this decision falls to be made, perhaps the many Lenzie folk who were proud to be styled 'Provost of Kirkintilloch' should not be forgotten.

There lingers on one further annoyance for Lenzie people, with regard to boundaries. The old divide still exists for parliamentary constituencies, resulting in South Lenzie being represented at Westminster by the Monklands West M.P. and North Lenzie by the M.P. for Strathkelvin & Bearsden. The local consensus seems to be that the latter should represent the whole of Lenzie. During the early 1980s an unsuccessful attempt was made by Lenzie residents to influence the Boundary Commission for Scotland over this matter.

Living in Lenzie

It would seem that people cannot feel entirely neutral about the concept of 'Living in Lenzie'. Residents of Lenzie are usually very positive about it, appreciating the excellent environment and amenities which exist there, but inhabitants of neighbouring communities are frequently less enthusiastic, either through sheer jealousy or – perhaps just as often – genuine cultural antipathy. And it has always been so, right from the start.

Perhaps it was because the first residents went out of their way to achieve different standards, inevitably distancing themselves from their near neighbours. The tone of a local newspaper report of June 1862 is revealing of the attitudes which prevailed in Lenzie, even at that early date:

> CAMPSIE JUNCTION. GRAND VOLUNTEER REVIEW.— On Saturday last a grand turn out of the 2nd Glasgow Regiment including the press and other corps took place in a field close to our station . . .Of our Campsie [sic] people there were many ladies present, and amongst the gentlemen we observed Messrs Nairn, Clugston, Mitchell, Muir and Field . . . We hope the Railway Directors will see that it is for their interest, to encourage such runs to the country, and if more of them can be attracted to our district, so much the better for all parties. Few places similarly situated can boast either of so many elegant villas,or of such a unanimous body of genteel families, in fact we question much if there is a place in Scotland which could take the shine out of Campsie Junction in these respects.

The alienation of some of the 'outsiders' is revealed in a letter published in the *Kirkintilloch Herald* of 4th May 1887, in which it was claimed that a *separate* celebration of Queen Victoria's Jubilee was being planned for the Lenzie working classes – 'twenty-three in all, comprising railway porters, sweeps, carpenters, painters, blacksmiths, gardeners, and Johnnie Broon' – at 12.00 noon, these being discounted from the 'Royal feast' at 5.00 pm:

> Why, sir, the working men of our country are its back-bone,the very essence of loyalty to our Queen, and her most noble defenders, while that modern middle-class conceit and presumption of the last twenty years' growth and in which such creatures exist, is an element in society ruinous to our country.

The letter may have been an outrageous libel, but the official 'Programme of Lenzie Celebration of Queen's Jubilee' reveals that 'Servants and Children and others in charge of children' were to be supplied with free refreshments in the Marquee at 1.30 pm, while at 6.00 pm there was to be a 'Dinner in Marquee for ladies and gentlemen' at a cost of five shillings per head, exclusive of wine.

However, in the middle of all the 'modern middle-class conceit and presumption' there existed in Lenzie a staunch tradition of radical liberalism, clear for all to recognise. John Ferguson was certainly regarded as a member of the 'lunatic left' by some of his contemporaries, while many of the other Lenzie stalwarts, including John Filshill, David Sandeman and A.C. Rutherford were staunch liberals. Ex-Provost David Perry caused a few raised eyebrows in 1914 when he lent his support not only to the Suffragettes, but to the Peace Movement as well.

One of the best attended Lenzie meetings of the Victorian era was that held on 8th September 1887 to inaugurate the Lenzie & Auchinloch Liberal Association. It was presided over by John Filshill and addressed by the famous R. B. Cunninghame Graham, M.P. for North-West Lanarkshire. Many prominent Lenzie residents were present, also the Rev. William Miller of the Union Church, and George Carlow, Stationmaster at Lenzie Station. Mr. John Frew moved 'That this meeting expresses its increased and increasing confidence in the statesmanship of the Right Hon. W. E. Gladstone, and pledges itself to support him in his policy for mutual self-government for Ireland', suggesting in passing that Gladstone might gain 'Home Rule for Scotland too, because they needed it . . . he had no doubt they would hear what had been heard before – the pibroch sounding through the land'. The motion was carried unanimously.

Vestiges of the Victorian liberal-radical tradition may still exist in Lenzie. Yet Lenzie nowadays returns two Conservative members to Strathkelvin District Council – the only two such members on the Council. Even neighbouring Bishopbriggs, with a similar social heritage deriving originally from the 'Villa Tickets' scheme, now returns no Conservative members at all from a one-time 'true-blue' locality. However, discussion of the twentieth-century social and political history of Lenzie lies outwith the remit of the present author. Perhaps some other scribe will tackle this interesting subject before long.

SOURCES OF LENZIE HISTORY

Most of the research of the present book has been carried out at the William Patrick Library, Kirkintilloch, using the varied range of primary and secondary resources in the Strathkelvin District Local Studies Collection. Of primary resources the most important by far are the official records of the Burgh of Kirkintilloch, especially minute books (including those of the 4th Ward Committee), valuation rolls, reports and correspondence. Other valuable archives include the records of the Lenzie Public Halls Trustees and the Cameron family papers. Census returns for Cadder and Kirkintilloch parishes are held for the years 1841, 1851, 1861, 1871 and 1881, on microfilm. Important typescript documents include *Lenzie: a Dissertation presented to the Mackintosh School of Architecture* (1980) by Derrick F. Milligan, *Strathkelvin Hospitals* (1986) by Derek A. Dow, and *Lenzie in Retrospect* by the late Ethel M. Lakeman. Miss Lakeman's essay gives marvellous insight into day-to-day life in a large Lenzie villa, early in the twentieth century.

Of published books, perhaps the most useful are two local histories: *Kirkintilloch: Town and Parish* (1894) by Thomas Watson, and *Life in a Scottish Country Town in the Victorian Era* (1940) by John Hillis, both of which give a good deal of information relating to Lenzie, although the dates given by Watson are frequently innaccurate. Information relating to the early history of the Edinburgh & Glasgow Railway can be found in *This Magnificent Line* (1986) by Allan P. McLean, and *The Springburn Story* (1964) by John Thomas. The history of the draining of Lenzie Loch will be found in *Agricultural Improvement in Strathkelvin 1700 - 1850* (1988) by Dorothy E. McGuire, while source information about housing in Lenzie is published in *Housing in Strathkelvin* (2 vols, 1989), edited by Jean D. Rae – especially in the sections dealing with 'Victorian Commuter Housing' and 'Inter-War Period Private Housing'. A quite excellent book, *Lenzie Academy, the First Hundred Years*, by John M. Reston, was published for the school's centenary in 1986. Centenary histories of all three Lenzie churches are available, as is *Gathered Leaves* (1925), an earlier book dealing with the Union Church. A *Centenary Brochure* of the Lenzie Bowling Club, published in 1973, has until now been the only available history of a Lenzie sporting club, but as the present book goes to press a quite lavishly produced history of the Golf Club, *100 Years off Lenzie Golf Club*, by Gordon Hislop, has just come to hand. Of colossal value are the indexed files of the *Kirkintilloch Herald*, held at the William Patrick Library, in microfilm, from 1886 onwards. For the period before 1886 files of the *Dumbarton Herald* and the *Lennox Herald* are most useful, but it is necessary to go to Dumbarton Library to consult these.

Of other 'external' sources the most useful are held in the different departments of the Scottish Record Office, in Edinburgh. In the 'Historical Search Room' of H.M. General Register House will be found complete runs of the valuation rolls of Cadder and Kirkintilloch parishes, from 1855 onwards, while at the West Search Room, Charlotte Square, one can see the minute books and other records of the Edinburgh & Glasgow and North British railways.

ACKNOWLEDGEMENTS

I am indebted to a great many Lenzie residents who have provided help, encouragement and inspiration during my researches. Especially: Mr. Donald Dickson, of Laurel Avenue, who as my history teacher at Lenzie Academy many years ago provided the initial spark which triggered my lifelong interest in local studies; John and Olive Cubbage, also of Laurel Avenue, whose perpetual enthusiasm for all matters relating to local history is a constant succour; Mr. James Leitch, of Kirkintilloch Road, who has given me access to his marvellous collection of old postcard views of Lenzie and has also provided a great deal of useful information; Miss Elizabeth Boyd, Mrs. Jenny MacPhedran, Mrs. Elsie Nelson and Mr. Ian Howie for their particular interest in the Lenzie Local History Project of 1989; and the many other residents who have completed questionnaires and loaned photographs in connection with the Project.

Two former Lenzie residents have deposited important documentary materials with Strathkelvin District Libraries: Miss L.V. Cameron (formerly of 'Blair Villa', Garngaber Avenue) has gifted many papers of local history interest, collected by members of the Cameron family, including documents and press cuttings relating to Lenzie; and Mr. Tom Lindsay (formerly of Middlemuir House, Douglas Avenue) has deposited the archives of the Lenzie Public Halls Trustees. Both of these deposits have proved invaluable during the present Project.

I am grateful to three professional colleagues, in particular, who have been of great assistance: Theresa Breslin, Librarian of Lenzie Library, who has helped with the research in many different ways, including the monotonous task of ploughing through old valuation rolls; Joe Fisher, Librarian of the Glasgow Room at the Mitchell Library – and denizen of the Mountain Moss! – who has helped me to track down portraits of many of the old Lenzie stalwarts in files of *The Bailie* periodical; and George Barbour, of the Scottish Record Office, who has helped to recover some elusive facts relating to the early history of Lenzie, from the British Rail archives at West Register House, Edinburgh.

Finally, a special mention of Eugene Duffy, for sterling photographic work; of Mr. James F. McEwan of Bearsden for information relating to the railway history of Lenzie; and of Mrs. Alice Mackenzie, of Garngaber Avenue, who when Chief Officer-Libraries & Museums of Strathkelvin initiated the Lenzie Local History Project and has maintained a keen interest since.

Kirkintilloch, 1989   Don Martin